A Course in Love

Powerful Teachings on Love, Sex, and Personal Fulfillment

Joan M. Gattuso

HarperSanFrancisco
An Imprint of HarperCollins*Publishers*

HarperCollins Web Site: http://www.harpercollins.com

HarperCollins® ▦®, and HarperSanFrancisco™
are trademarks of HarperCollins Publishers Inc.

Library of Congress Cataloging-in-Publication Data

Gattuso, Joan M.
   A Course in Love : a self-discovery guide to finding your
soulmate / Joan M. Gattuso.
     ISBN 0–06–251301–X (cloth)
     ISBN 0–06–251301–8 (pbk.)
     1. Love. 2. Man-woman relationships. I. Title.
HQ801.G37 1996
646.7'7 – dc20   95–33426

96 97 98 99 00 ❖ HAD 10 9 8 7 6 5 4 3 2

From my heart and soul
this book is lovingly dedicated to
my husband and soulmate,
David S. Alexander,
who was worth the wait.

Contents

The Knowing

The memory lies in us of how it could be in a loving relationship with one another, how it could be holy, filled with gentleness, kissed by heaven. And that love could be extended to everyone.

There is somewhere within each of us a place where we remember and we know. It may have become but a faint whisper today, but when we are quiet, we hear it still.

Through all the madness that has been perpetrated in the name of love, through the dysfunctional patterns and tears and fears, beneath it all lies this ancient knowing. We are not here to do battle and create a hell out of God's holy ground; we are here to love one another, to experience heaven here together.

Acknowledgments

There are people in my life who have made the journey richer, sweeter, and more challenging, and to whom I wish to express my gratitude:

To all those who have so long supported me and believed in me—especially my parents, Jim and Vivian; my brothers Jim and Perry; my longtime friends Susy Miller Schwabe, Ginna Bell Bragg, Nancy Miller, Pat McClain, and Roger Goins—thanks for your love through my years of drama and into the present.

To Sandy Daleiden, David's friend who "knew" I was his soulmate.

To John Broad, who had the courage to speak to what he saw in me and saved my life, and to Ronn Liller.

To Felicia Hyde-Martinez, our church administrative assistant, who always gives 100 percent and who picked up many pieces so that I would be able to write.

To Kim Cahuas, my wonderful business manager.

To my stepdaughters Robyn, Lisa, and Julie and their families. You are a tremendous blessing, and I thank you for accepting me so totally.

To my Master Mind partner, Marleen Davis.

To Linda Spencer, my soul sister and fellow sojourner on the path, who prayed for me without ceasing, who believed in me and the message of this book, and who celebrated each step with me.

To my spiritual teachers Sister Augustine, O.P., Joyce Kramer, Martha Giudici, Dennis Adams, Dr. Jean Houston, and His Holiness the Dalai Lama.

To my loving and conscious congregation, Unity of Greater Cleveland.

To Marianne Williamson, who helped birth the idea of this book in October 1992, and Wayne Dyer, who nurtured the idea along in December 1992. You two fanned the flame and the idea became a reality.

To Dan Wakefield, my guardian angel. You have blessed my life beyond measure.

To my literary agent, Anne Sibbald, for saying yes. You are the perfect one.

To the ideal staff at Harper San Francisco, especially editor Lisa Bach for taking on this project in midstream and doing such an excellent job and Barbara Moulton for your belief in the message and your enthusiasm for getting it out.

To Joel Fotinos, marketing manager, a kindred spirit whose passion for this project is my blessing.

To those who helped me learn the importance of forgiveness and to those who taught me what love really is. I thank you all.

Acknowledgments

And from the depth of my being to Joan Kirkwood Miley, who years ago was my secretary, who always believed in me and my message, who gave to me and this project countless hours over the last two years, who made sense out of my handwritten stream of consciousness. I thank you for giving so much and for your encouragement, love, friendship, and support. You are a treasure and a dear friend.

To my husband, David S. Alexander—the love of my life, soulmate, gift from God, and still my very best manifestation of Spiritual Principle—for your love and willingness to do whatever was needed to assist me in birthing this book. I am eternally grateful.

To the Holy Spirit for the years of inspiration and guidance, and for the love that enfolds me in all that I do.

A Course in Love

Introduction

David was ten when he knew. I was older, perhaps fourteen, when I knew.

We knew the *possibility* of being in a loving relationship in which one's soul draws to itself its perfect partner. This partner would not fill our empty place, but would perfectly complement the fullness of our inner selves, our spirits.

As children in small-town middle America in the fifties and sixties, we did not have many role models for such a loving and fulfilling relationship. As the two of us passed through puberty, there certainly was no mention of being with one's soulmate and having a joyful partnership. But we knew that there was a remarkable way in which to be in a relationship, and we would not stop the quest until that way was found.

The prevailing message to women of that day was that men were to be tolerated at best. The common belief was,

"Can't live with 'em and can't live without 'em." Most men were saying the same thing about women. Both camps in the battle of the sexes were fortified with enough anger, hostility, unmet expectations, and cruelty to keep the war going for years. Most relationships were, and still are, about doing battle with each other in an attempt to manipulate the partner into fulfilling our unmet needs.

Yet the flame of another possibility continued to burn, and in the face of no tangible evidence to support this inner certainty, it stayed with us. Through two early and unfortunate marriages, it stayed with me. This was true for David as well. He also experienced two marriages that ended in divorce.

In my soul I knew relationships were meant to be holy, not hell. Loving another meant loving him all the time, not just when he was doing what I wanted him to do or saying what I wanted him to say. Love had to be unconditional or it wasn't love. Being together would be easy, not work. We would naturally be kind and considerate of each other. To behave otherwise would be unnatural. We would be comfortable together. We would have a great deal in common and respect each other's differences. Our essences would connect.

As Leslie Parrish Bach says in her husband Richard Bach's book *A Bridge Across Forever,* "A soulmate is someone who has locks that fit our keys, and keys to fit our locks. When we feel safe enough to open the locks, our truest selves step out and we can be completely and honestly who we are, we can be loved for who we are and not for who we're pretending to be."

We would know God together. The sexual aspect would be easy and pleasurable but would only be a piece of the magnificence. Our love would embrace other people rather than exclude them as a threat to our relationship. Such a relationship would bring a touch of heaven to our daily lives.

Elizabeth Bowen wrote, "Certain books come to meet one, as do people." A spiritual text entitled *A Course in Miracles* came to meet me in November 1976. I fully agree with Marianne Williamson's description of *A Course in Miracles* as "a self-study program of spiritual psychotherapy." As I began to study the *Course* in depth, my soul resonated with the spiritual teachings it contained. Although the material was similar to what I had been coming to know was true through my study of Unity's teachings and through meditation, it brought every aspect of life into clear focus. *A Course in Miracles* is the foundation of my spiritual understanding. Its instruction on relationships, and its affirmation of how glorious they can be, is clearer and better than anything else I have encountered.

When I began studying and applying these spiritual principles, I stepped onto a new path, a path that led me into a number of trainings, teachings, and spiritual adventures. My life began to radically transform, and I began to view all of life from a different point of view, seeing relationships in a way that I had never been taught.

What I had known in my soul to be true was now being confirmed in these teachings: it *is* possible to have love without conflict, to totally forgive the past, to have happiness as the purpose of relationships, to know that relationships were meant to be holy. I held to these truths and began an incredible journey of transformation. That journey and what could be yours is presented to you in *A Course in Love*.

In the first part of this book, we will look at the status of most relationships today. An honest, thoughtful examination of our relationships suggests that nearly all of us have settled for the dysfunctional norm: relationships born out of the ego rather than the spirit.

The second part of the book moves beyond the unacceptable norm to what is possible in our relationships. The journey from hell to holy relationships is laid out step-by-step so that you, the reader, can take this journey and create your own transformational relationship.

The journey's end — a holy relationship — is the subject of the final section. What does a holy, transformational relationship look like? What makes two people soulmates? In this section, I share my miraculous story of meeting my soulmate and how our love drew us together through time and space. We will also take an intimate look at the blessed unions of several other couples who enjoy successful, love-filled relationships. Included is a list of the common factors found in the expression of love between soulmates. If you are not already in a holy relationship, you will find all the tools necessary to transform the repetitive patterns of failed relationships into relationships that are easy, joyous, energizing, loving, happy, healthy, and free.

I took hold of the spiritual principles taught in *A Course in Miracles* and, with my own spiritual faith, applied them unceasingly to my life and history. I learned to rise out of victim consciousness into self-mastery, out of fear, hurt, and separation into love, peace, and bliss.

I've done it. So can you. It's much more than a possibility. It's the way life was meant to be. If you also hold what I term "the knowing" within your heart, I share with you from Richard Bach's treasure, *Illusions:* "You are never given a wish without also being given the power to make it true. You may have to work for it, however."

On July 25, 1986, my soulmate and I met and began walking together to God. This is our story of spiritual quickening and of bringing what the heart knows is true into living, breathing expression.

Getting here wasn't easy, but David was worth the wait and the work. It is my prayer and sincerest desire that you too may know love in a life-supporting, renewing way.

There is a way the world looks at relationships that does not work. There is a way to look at relationships that truly does work, and I have found it. Now you too can have true love.

1

Relationships: Holy or Hell?

Sam and Kathy met in graduate school, where he was a student and she was in administration. They were friends for quite a while and eventually began dating casually, which soon led to their dating each other exclusively.

Initially, one could not praise the other's virtues loudly enough. Sam told his family and his buddies that he had finally met the woman for him. She personified everything he wanted in a wife. She was a beautiful blonde and had a rewarding career, but she was willing to put his career and possible moves ahead of her own goals. She had a cutting wit and thought his humor was charming. She was athletic and loved their home sports teams as much as he did. She could take care of herself, and he just knew she would take good care of him.

Kathy, on the other hand, had just ended a five-year relationship with a man who was incapable of making a commitment.

At the time that Sam began pursuing her more directly, Kathy was tired of being "the one who keeps giving and giving. Next time I'm going to choose someone who wants to give to me."

Kathy enjoyed Sam's company, and they shared many interests, as well as similar career goals. She knew that in time she could help Sam change those few characteristics of his that she did not like or found irritating.

At this point the warning signs were already evident. Here are some of the obvious ones that ultimately would doom Sam and Kathy's relationship:

- Sam's first mention of Kathy to his friends always had to do with her looks—"beautiful and blond."
- Kathy was willing to put Sam's goals ahead of hers.
- Sam knew that Kathy would take good care of him.
- Kathy had recently ended a troubled relationship.
- Kathy expected to "help Sam change."

Later we will explore in depth why these signs point to a relationship that will evolve into conflict, suffering, and failure. For now, just examine these early warning signs as they may apply to your own relationship.

Sam and Kathy's romance was on-again, off-again for a couple of years, but all their friends could see that they truly cared for each other and had a "special" relationship.

A Course in Miracles teaches a radical view of what "special" means. Specialness is seen not as something wonderful, loving, and positive, but rather as something that isolates us and fills us with fear—fear that at any second what we perceive as love and the union of two souls will be snatched away. While living in a consciousness of specialness, we view all others as separate and apart from us, fiercely denying through our beliefs and actions our underlying oneness.

When seen clearly, special relationships can be viewed as codependent, compulsive relationships. Held together by the ego, these unhealthy alliances are doomed to fail. We must realize that "special" is a poor substitute for what could be. We have accepted specialness, which separates and causes pain, in place of holiness, which joins and brings love.

Specialness is not love. It is a substitute for love. When two lovers are in a special relationship, an impenetrable wall remains forever between them, keeping each one separate and apart, lonely and isolated.

While in specialness we are ever ready to assume the role of judge, jury, and executioner to our lover for any behavior or attitude that does not correspond to our image of how he or she is supposed to be. Specialness continues to live only through the defeat of our former lover, through devaluing, judging, or discounting him or her.

Consider the times you have dismissed as unworthy or insignificant a person you once claimed to love or whom you at least cared for deeply. That's specialness in action. Here are some red flags of a special relationship:

- You care for someone for what he or she can give you, for example, name, home, security, children, wealth, sex.
- You feel a need to rescue the other person.
- A lover quickly turns into an enemy.
- What you once called love soon becomes disdain or even hate.
- The physical aspect of the relationship is of utmost importance.

- Bodies are everything; essence is not very important. You focus on the outer package and never examine the inner essence.
- You feel the need to remake your partner, giving the message that he or she is not good enough the way he or she is right now.
- You always point out what is lacking in the partner.
- The relationship is filled with judgments, guilt, hurt, and anger.
- You always hold the "object of your love" at arm's length to be reviewed or scrutinized.
- You trust no one except yourself.
- Almost from the beginning of a new relationship you start to give up parts of what makes you unique.
- You make constant comparisons, attempting to establish your worth by devaluing your partner.
- You regard others as either beneath you or above you because you focus on people's differences rather than their similarities.
- Through specialness you are ever ready to attack, find fault, adjust, make over, correct, or alter in some "helpful" way.
- You look to your partner to fulfill your needs.
- You see the other person as an object, rather than as brother or sister, someone just like you.
- You place limits on love.
- A little whisper you do not like, a circumstance that does not suit you, an unexpected event—any of these can upset your fragile world, hurling you into chaos.
- Your relationship is threatened by everything.

Our individual lists of specialness can take myriad forms, but the underlying thoughts and feelings are always clashing with our divine heritage and adamantly denying the depth of love that could be experienced. The end result, no matter what form of expression it takes, is always the same—pain! We choose specialness instead of peace, specialness instead of heaven, specialness instead of true love.

The idea that the root cause of suffering in relationships is the desire for specialness can be traced back twenty-five hundred years to the teachings of the two renowned Chinese philosophers, Lao-tzu and Chuang-tzu, the fathers of Taoism. They understood that all our woes occur because we create a separateness and specialness for ourselves. When we separate ourselves from others, we are in conflict with them. Our desire for specialness is why we suffer.

Sam and Kathy did move to another part of the country where Sam had a terrific opportunity for business advancement. Kathy quite willingly gave up her successful and rewarding career to move. In their new location she was unable to find a similar position. For several months she worked as a temporary staffer, but this immediately bored her and she grew increasingly dissatisfied.

Eventually she joined Sam in his business, and together they built a successful enterprise. By all outward appearances their life together looked great, but underneath the veneer of specialness major conflicts were brewing.

Kathy felt a lot of resentment toward Sam because of the move that had required her to give up a gratifying career. His own career contentment became more and more irritating to her. She no longer felt much of a connection with Sam. When she tried to discuss her feelings with him, he'd just make a joke and tell her he felt great and there was no problem. Flashbacks of her previous painful relationship kept coming to Kathy. She felt as if she were beginning to relive her past.

Many real and deep problems continued to rise to the surface in what had appeared to be a happy relationship. At the time, neither Sam nor Kathy had the tools or the wisdom to successfully resolve these conflicts. After a couple of years of each one coming from the position of, "If only you'd change, everything would be okay between us," both were emotionally drained. Sam didn't want to change those characteristics Kathy viewed as irritating. In fact, Kathy's constant nagging about them became an extreme irritation to Sam. The situation continued to deteriorate until Kathy and Sam separated and then divorced.

For Sam and Kathy, the end result of eight years of ego struggles, breakups, and makeups was a divorce after only three years of marriage.

Their story is not unique. The divorce rate in the United States is not at 50 percent because we are all experts in creating loving, supportive, lasting relationships. What most of us know how to do is short-term romance or flings. We play nice just as long as our ego-based needs are met. When these needs are no longer fulfilled, most folks pack their bags and run—if not physically, then emotionally and mentally. That is, we may stay for fifty years but lead lives of "quiet desperation," as Thoreau put it. All of us know couples who fit this description. Maybe you feel this describes you.

Whenever we are in a relationship based on what we can get rather than what we can be, do, and give, it is "special" and will not last. Special relationships are the American model. We come together as two wounded, unhealed people who hope to get our needs met. Most likely, we do not recognize the true dynamics of the situation and may never identify the real problem.

A special relationship is our attempt to relive the past and this time have a different outcome. This kind of relationship is based on ego needs and not on love. We may call it love, but it is not. When we exist in this kind of partnership, we always see the flaws of others, especially our mate's. If only he or she would do this, be that, say this, then my life would work. I would be happy. We project our ability to be happy onto our partners and expect them to make us happy, fulfill our needs, and live according to our expectations.

The reaction to this situation is predictable. When your mate meets your needs, then you think you're happy and fulfilled. When your mate falls short of your expectations, you feel betrayed and empty. The truth of the situation is that after the initial glow begins to dim, your needs and expectations cannot possibly be met and you become miserable. She becomes the source of your misery. He's behaving selfishly. She's thoughtless even though you've given so much to her. Meanwhile, he's complaining to his buddies about you and your excessive demands and even worse, your dwindling interest in sex. You feel unloved, he feels unloved; neither of you is getting your needs met, and neither is going to.

Couples often become entangled in a web of bartering (If you meet my needs, I will do what you want, be what you want) and keeping score (Who last did what for whom?). But this will not work. It cannot work because love is not a trade-off.

What Your Parents Couldn't Teach You

One of the most important lessons about relationships was never taught to you in school. If you had been so instructed, it would have served you well. Your mother and father never taught you either, but only because they did not know. They were never taught by their parents. Here it is. Pay attention and think about it. *No one can fulfill your needs but you.* No one! We'll search on and on, never quite finding the right one. We keep believing that if only we could find the right person, all our problems would cease.

Accept it! For it is the truth. No one can meet your needs but you. You can cry about it, rage about it, pout and scream about it, but the result will be the same if you don't live by it—misery. You can try to coerce and manipulate, seek to compromise, or even make yourself physically ill, but the result does not change. Two unhappy people will still be lost, unhealed, and miserable if they believe it is the other person's responsibility to meet their needs and make them happy.

Seeking and not finding is the game of the ego. We are forever seeking outside ourselves for an answer that can only be found within. We desperately want to find it in the outside world. We continue to insist that it must be there, but it is not. The sooner we can comprehend that what we are looking for is not to be found outside ourselves, the sooner we can get off the merry-go-round of failed relationships and move forward. No one can give you what you are unwilling to give yourself.

In a special relationship, each party keeps portions of herself or himself separate from the other. Within each lurks an overwhelming fear that if the partner were ever to see what lies deep within, he or she would recoil in terror. The truth of a special relationship is that we do not love ourselves enough to be able to truly love another.

We've all heard, "Love your neighbor as yourself." Most of us have never learned to love ourselves, so how can we love our neighbor, our lover, our husband or wife? We've been given so many screwed-up, false messages about love that for most of us love has become a fantasy, a word from long ago never to be realized.

Our insistence on specialness keeps us from realizing the will of God in our relationships. God's will for us is always to know love. God's love is given equally to each of us. In this love we have free will to decide whether we accept love's message now or at some distant future time. Until we accept the ways of true love, there remains in us a knowledge, however faint, that specialness will not give us what we truly want or recognize who we truly are.

Instead of living a heaven on earth, as God's love would have it be, we have created a hell here and now and called it home. While in specialness, we are asleep, surrounded by a world of loveliness we do not see. Living in the world that specialness creates is like living in a bad dream and not knowing it is a dream. We stamp our feet, insisting within the dream that it is reality. If we are to free ourselves from the damaging effects of specialness, we must be willing to question every value we hold dear. This can be a terrifying process that can cause egos to go berserk.

In looking back over the years of my spiritual awakening and soul growth, I can now clearly see that each step was necessary and essential, but during the various stages, especially the early ones, this certainly was not evident. I stepped onto this path kicking and screaming, insisting that I still wanted to do it my way. It took years for me to understand that maybe, just maybe, God had a better way. Just possibly, God had a purpose for our being together in the type of partnership that I had intuitively known about as a teenager but had never experienced.

As a minister I have officiated at many weddings. Being with couples during this joyous time, I find it interesting to observe their personal dynamics. Happily, most seem very connected with each other. Others, though, are much more concerned with the exterior trappings than with what is actually happening. I've seen grooms still trying to please a domineering mother and brides sobbing hysterically moments before we are to begin. Everyone always says it's nerves, but I sense it is much more. I too was once a sobbing young bride, absolutely knowing that the long walk down the aisle wearing the expensive gown in the cavernous church was a big mistake. I too swallowed the knowing and walked.

I pray I will only be asked to officiate at weddings of couples truly connected and never asked to marry those who are not. Sometimes that has not been the case.

One Saturday I ran into one of the brides from the previous year at a local department store. I remembered Shannon instantly: a petite, beautiful young woman who looked just like the bride doll on the top of her cake. Her wedding will always be clearly fixed in my memory. It was 104 degrees and the ceremony was held outside. There were moments when I thought the entire wedding party was going to topple forward on cue. Asking how she and Andrew were, I was stunned when she replied, "Divorced!" Divorced within the first year. I don't know the details of Shannon and Andrew's story, but as with many other couples, it hadn't taken long for their ego-backed demands to get out of control. What was once "special" love quickly turned to "special" hate.

Ann and Tim had a "special" relationship from the start. He was older and authoritative, the molder, and she was young and pliable, or so he thought. Ann was willing, initially, to do anything and be anything to please Tim. She had just recently, painfully, ended her first marriage after that husband announced he was leaving her to marry a man. Needless to say,

Ann felt a tremendous sense of rejection. Her self-confidence plummeted.

Tim quickly set a course for Ann, controlling her diet, exercise, reading, studying, vitamin intake, and wardrobe selection. Perhaps he fancied himself as Professor Higgins from *My Fair Lady*, but Ann was no Eliza. Ann rebelled and they divorced. Tim instantly went into a third marriage and soon began having an affair with Ann. She no longer wanted to be made over, but she was addicted to his domineering yet charming demeanor and sexual prowess. She was in the snare of the classic special relationship and seemed emotionally unable to live without him.

Whenever you believe you cannot live without another person, *watch out*. The belief that your very life depends on another person is a clear warning that the relationship is unhealthy. So what do most of us do? We boldly walk straight into it. You know we do. You've probably done it. I've done it. Nearly everyone we know has done it.

So what do you think Ann and Tim did? He divorced wife number three and Ann and Tim remarried. It was a remarriage filled with the promise that this time everything would be different. Of course it wasn't. It couldn't be, because they were no different than before. They were still the same two wounded souls they had been six years ago. They did not change simply by mouthing the words "I'll change." Change simply does not happen just because we say so. To truly change, to transform an old negative pattern into a new supportive one takes a great deal of willingness, commitment, and work. It never happens simply because we want it.

This time was not exactly the same as before with Ann and Tim. This time it got worse. Physical violence erupted when she was no longer willing to be molded into his plaything. He continued with his affairs, and the relationship failed. Was the failed relationship his fault? No. Was it her fault? No. Both Ann and Tim were living with emotional wounds, wounds that went so deep into their souls that they constantly got in the way of Ann and Tim's ability to be truly with each other.

Finding who is to blame isn't helpful. Finding the underlying soul wounds within the psyche that attracted such a relationship is.

What initially attracted Tim to Ann was exactly what he wanted to change as the relationship developed. In a special relationship what first attracts us is exactly what we later want to change. If a partner is extremely outgoing and vivacious and we say, "How wonderful! He has such an open personality and is so much fun," we will later feel threatened by this same personality and will be critical of his never being serious enough. In a special relationship a woman who is meticulous about herself and her home, and is at first much admired for her efforts, will later be criticized by her partner for taking so much time to get ready or keep up the house or for being unable to relax.

It doesn't take much to upset the precarious balance of such relationships. Anything and everything can quickly come between the partners in these dysfunctional, ego-ruled alliances.

The problem for Tim and Ann lay in the fact that these two basically decent human beings were both filled with their own oozing wounds and had been unwilling to acknowledge them. Denial of our problems does not make them go away. Actually, they only fester and worsen as we deny them.

Ann finally woke up and realized that this was a very non-supportive, unhealthy way to be living her life. She left the relationship and began her own emotional recovery. She now knows, several years later, that an unhealed piece of her is still drawn to Tim and men like him. She is attracted to men who want to daddy her or remake her, men who think she's wonderful but aren't quite satisfied with her. She's working on resolving that. As for Tim, he's now married to wife number five. Please note that Ann left the relationship and then began working on why and how she got there. The first thing a woman in a physically abusive relationship must do is get out and seek help immediately. It may be the most difficult step a battered woman ever takes, but it is the most necessary.

The "specialness" of Ann's relationship was at times disguised as love. At other times it seemed to offer hope, but all the while it was predisposed to have condemnation as its goal. At some time we have all cut a very bad deal. We have traded off love for specialness, choosing to see each other as bodies rather than as spiritual beings, focusing more on what we can get from a partner than on who he or she is. We are looking outside for answers that can only be found within ourselves.

We are like the man who one night is searching under a streetlight for his key. A stranger passes by and asks what the fellow is looking for. He responds, "My key," and the second fellow joins in the search. Unsuccessful at finding the key, the second man asks the first, "Exactly where were you standing when you dropped the key?" "Oh, I was standing in the house, but the electricity is off, so I came out here to search under the light of the lamppost."

The key isn't out there. It wasn't lost out there, and it isn't going to be found out there. But by God, how we do try to insist that it is there. Many spend a lifetime searching for the answer outside while it sits in the center of the soul and waits.

Special relationships always involve a great deal of pain—not just emotional or physical pain, but pain that goes through the psyche and into the soul. While we are in the throes of a special relationship, that knowing part of us does not disappear. It is gently instructing us that there is another way to be in partnership, a way that does not demand sacrifice and pain, which we must then convince ourselves is love.

Sacrifice: An Important Piece of the Puzzle

What a dreadful and manipulative word *sacrifice* is. It took me many years to learn that sacrifice comes only from fear and not out of love. And, as we all know, fearful people can be vicious. Sacrifice then becomes attack and does not resemble love. When I learned that, I knew I had at long last found a piece to my puzzle.

Nearly all the popular psychology of the day espouses some form of sacrifice. It may be called compromise or negotiation, but it's still sacrifice. It doesn't work. Whenever you feel you must sacrifice some aspect of yourself or your life, you will end up resentful and angry. You will feel like the loser and set a course to win next time. Everyone loses in the game of sacrifice.

The mere idea of sacrifice is out of alignment with spiritual truth. God did not initiate the sacrifice of your spirit, essence, and uniqueness. The whole idea of sacrifice is a human creation. Sacrifice is not spiritual. It is not God's way, but it certainly is the ego's way.

The notion of sacrifice has controlled people, women especially, through the ages. Women have denied their aspirations and dreams, snuffed out their great passions. Women have traditionally had the role of nurturers, but unfortunately most have never learned to nurture themselves. The result has been the creation of a lot of very angry people. Do without for someone else's supposed good, be it your partner's, your children's, or your nation's, and then honestly evaluate how you feel. You feel put upon, deprived of your worth, angry, and then guilty for having those feelings. Sacrifice produces guilt in us as surely as love produces peace.

Sacrifice will get you nowhere. There is always a way out of conflict and disagreement in your relationship, but sacrifice, yours or the other person's, surely isn't it. If you have believed that sacrifice is love, I ask you to consider sacrifice as not being an expression of love, but rather as separation from love. Sacrifice does not draw us closer together; it pushes in a little farther the wedge between us.

Initially, it is nearly impossible to conceive of love without sacrifice, since the connection of the two is so pervasive in our culture. The notion of sacrifice is born out of the idea that there is not enough—not enough love, kindness, thoughtfulness, opportunities, time, money, caring, fun, pleasure, beauty, enjoyment.

Whatever the perceived good might be, the idea of sacrifice says there isn't enough good for everyone to have some. It is the notion that we live in a world of scarcity, that we must give up what little we have in order for another to have anything at all. Sacrifice is a family of five sitting down to dinner with four servings on the table. The mother says, "Oh, it doesn't matter. I'm not hungry. You can have mine." Meanwhile, she's exhausted and starving. We have all denied ourselves our rightful serving and said, "It doesn't matter," when it did. It mattered a lot! Just because the idea of sacrifice is everywhere does not mean that it is true. Each time we believe sacrifice is called for, we are denying who we are and who God is.

A Course in Miracles teaches that our confusion of sacrifice with love is so profound that we cannot conceive of love without sacrifice. It is this notion that we must look at; we must come to understand that "sacrifice is attack, not love." The teaching continues, "If you would accept this one idea, your fear of love would vanish."

In the game of sacrifice there are always seeming winners and losers. In the game of love everyone gets to be a winner. It took me a long while to understand that. When I was living in mental and emotional confusion while in a special relationship, I thought that if I gave up who I was, I would get the love I desired.

All of us seem to excel at creating our own dramas and outrageous situations. I have come to understand these dramas as our desperate attempts to get the attention of our innermost self. One of my worst nightmares follows.

The Monster Driving the Steamroller at You; Or Do I Have Your Attention Now?

My friends in Alcoholics Anonymous speak of alcohol being like an elephant in the living room. Everyone in an alcoholic's household tiptoes around the elephant, never mentioning its presence, pretending it isn't there. All the while it is dominating the life of every family member, not just that of the alcoholic.

I have noticed that many of us have an elephant or even a monster living in our household, and we attempt to pretend it isn't there. This monster is always an outer manifestation of unresolved inner fears. Fear is the great destroyer of relationships, dooming them to failure even before they have begun. Fear can quickly turn our special love into a special hate. Fear lives in the heart, mind, and experiences, but it does not exist of its own accord. Even though it often seems otherwise, fear itself has no life. It exists only when we give it life. Fear is a parasitic thought, which, as we feed and nourish it, appears to take on a life of its own. Fear is then able to take over our lives. Fear is a monster so hideous that you and I deny any association with it in our attempt to keep it from penetrating our conscious awareness.

In most instances, our unresolved, unhealed fears are so enormous that, even when love is gifted to us, we are unable to receive it because fear has barricaded our hearts. My monster was so destructive and enormous that it rampaged through my life driving a steamroller.

Perhaps, someday, we will all be able to look back at our lives and clearly perceive a turning point, a point where we made a decision that would forever change the direction of our lives. My point of change came the night before leaving for California to officiate at my lifelong friend Ginna's wedding. I had not known until that day that my then husband, with whom I had a fear-filled, special relationship, had discovered a small reserve of cash I had been squirreling away. I was planning to leave him just as soon as I could save enough money to afford my own place.

His discovery of my hidden cash tipped him off that I was indeed planning to leave him—maybe even that very day. We had had some very fearful, insane scenes before, but nothing like that night. I was right on the edge of an emotional breakdown and yet knew that my hysteria would only fuel his raging behavior. Through prayer and the grace of God I made it through that night as he first hurled my packed suitcase against the wall, its contents flying about the room, and then grabbed me around the neck and held me down on the bed, making terrifying threats. My life had turned into a nightmare. Me, a spiritual teacher, in the throes of domestic violence. I was frozen in fear. I was traumatized. I had become a battered woman.

Why? Why had I stayed so long? This was it! My fear for my life was clearly greater than my fear of a second divorce, my fear of starting over and being on my own again. Why? How had I let it get so far?

I had shut down to love and knew it. I tried to pray, but I was so traumatized that all I could say was, "Help! Help me, God!" Then later I was able to add, "I promise I will never put myself in this insanity again. Get me through this night, and I will work on healing my soul and go on."

In the midst of my trauma, two messages from *A Course in Miracles* began to repeat over and over in my head: "Only perfect love exists" and "Only love is real." In the several weeks leading up to that fateful night, I had been studying these two teachings but had not been quite able to understand them. That night, even in my fear, I finally recognized the truth contained within these two lines.

Only love is real. From deep within my soul I was remembering a lesson learned long ago. In all of life, in all of the world, so much that appears to be real isn't. It is a brief, fleeting circumstance. It lacks substance. It is nothing more than a ripple in the great ocean of life.

The only reality is love. Love is not fleeting or brief; it is eternal. Love is the pulse of the universe.

It was as if a soul strength or knowledge buried within me was being called forth from the depths of my being. If I was experiencing fear, and I was, then I was experiencing something of my own making and not of God's creation. God creates only perfect love, which is real. As Buddha taught, fear is unreal, impermanent, and thus can be called an illusion. I can make a fearful mess, which in the truest sense can be said to be unreal, because God didn't create it. And only what is divine is real and lasting. Everything else is impermanent and changing.

From then on I clung to these two truths—only love is real; only perfect love exists—whenever my enraged ego would rail at me that fear was real and that attempting to give it up was crazy.

Only love is real. I knew this was the truth. I also knew that I did not understand it, but I was willing to do whatever was necessary to understand. There are always signs to tell us whether we are doing the right thing or making the right decision. Fear is a signal of the strain that arises when our desires conflict with our actions. Listening to our personal egos, we often choose actions that conflict with our ultimate good. We ignore the obvious signs telling us to slow down or to go ahead or to turn right.

What I came to understand was that my inner essence, my spirit and soul, had been attempting for quite some time to get me to wake up and move on with my life. I hadn't been willing to pay attention. In the web of confusion in which I was caught, I thought that my former husband was my good, or that he somehow possessed my good and wasn't giving it to me. What I came to understand through the healing of my soul was that God not only has my good, God is my good.

The scene that night got my attention. Soon afterward I became willing to look not only at the fear it produced, but at all I had feared in life. I began to experience life from an entirely different point of view, moving out of victim consciousness and into being the victor.

The beginning was slow. First I learned to crawl, then to take tiny baby steps, then to walk on my own, and finally to soar.

I was praying for a healed relationship with my former husband. I believed if I loved enough, the relationship would be healed. I finally came to love enough. I loved myself enough to flee from a physically threatening and emotionally scarring environment.

After that terrifying night, I was finally miserable enough to get out and do some deep, introspective work. I was finally willing to do whatever was needed to deal with the core beliefs I carried that had caused the effects I was experiencing.

Discomfort helps us become aware of the need for correction. Well, I was pretty darned uncomfortable. It could definitely be said that my discomfort level was up! Isn't it curious how we have to have our backs against the wall, our lives flashing in front of us, before we are willing to change? I became willing to begin, right there, to perceive the situation differently.

To perceive differently is to see an old situation in a new light—to see the gory details of your past relationship as a lesson held out to you rather than as karma, a punishment, or a payback. We can get so caught up in the excruciating details, the telling and the retelling, that we miss the lesson. Each lesson in life that we miss is presented again and again until we get it. Go back and look at the significant events of your life. See if you don't discover a pattern. The names, faces, and events may vary, but the underlying script is the same.

I have noticed that, with each repetition, the intensity of the situation increases. The earlier lesson levels were obviously not powerful enough to get our attention. We miss the first several road signs of life because we are in such a fog. Then, the signs and signals get bigger, with flashing neon lights and waving banners. For some of us, as the signs and signals get bigger, our denial of any problem grows proportionately larger. And on and on the insanity goes.

"My God, what's happening?" we cry out. Many people conclude that God is punishing them. They project the responsibility for their situation onto a distant, stern, revengeful deity. What's really happening is that our soul has agreed to the creation of our particular monster in the living room. It has done this in an attempt to bring the necessity for correction into our consciousness.

Once we realize that whatever is occurring is happening through us and not to us, then and only then can we do anything about our relationship problems. As long as you stay in the belief that everything is happening to you, you will stay in a helpless, hopeless, victim state. Life can be heaven. Why do you insist on making it hell? You have given your power to the negative situation rather than to your own inner, invincible spirit. Once you wake up and take personal charge of cleaning up your negative beliefs and patterns, nothing can stop you. You will proceed undaunted.

What I needed to do with my former husband, with whom I had had a special relationship, was not to shoot him, but to forgive him. Discomfort is aroused only to bring the need for correction into awareness. Look at all the discomforting circumstances and events in your life. Instead of viewing them as happening to you, begin to see them as happening through you as a means of getting you to perceive how great is the need for correction within you.

Mild, sweet, gentle circumstances seldom get our attention. On the other hand, there's nothing quite like a monster driving a steamroller at you to get your attention.

2

Do You Love Me or My Body?

I recall seeing a beautiful entertainer speaking about losing her "new mommy tummy" after the birth of her last child. Mind you, this woman left the hospital in a regular size 6. So after a couple of months of dieting and daily workouts with a personal trainer, she's feeling pretty darn good about her physical appearance. Now her husband hasn't said a word about any of this. I think, Good for him—he loves her no matter what shape her body is in.

So the evening comes for her first professional appearance since giving birth, and she is wearing a long slinky number and feeling pretty fabulous. She coyly asks her spouse, "Honey, how do you think I look? Does my tummy look flat enough?"

So he answers, "Well, actually you still do have a bit of a pot—try to suck it in. You'll probably need to lose three or four more pounds to look like you did before the baby."

This woman is now a size 4. She never needed to lose an ounce to look or be fabulous. She was already gorgeous. Another way her husband could have responded, if he had been able to see her as more than her body, would have gone something like this: "Flat enough! You always look magnificent. I care about you, your essence. It is your inner beauty radiating through your entire being that makes you such a knockout, not the size of your hips."

Does this mean we are supposed to lie about how we see someone? No, not lie, but it does mean we need to open our eyes a little more and see beyond the narrow margins of our bodies.

Many people today have attempted to turn the body into God. Most give far more time and devotion and money to its care, pampering, and shaping than is ever given to the spiritual aspect of life. We view ourselves as only our bodies. Others view us as only our bodies. We view others as only their bodies.

This cultural obsession contributes mightily to perpetuating "special" relationships. Just as long as we continue to view ourselves and others as bodies is how long we shall continue to experience a sense of alienation and disconnection with the true self and with the inner essence of another.

So many people have spoken to me about how they hate their bodies. I have noticed that this so-called hatred has nothing to do with their state of physical health or muscle tone. The hatred stems from a judgmental perception that says, No matter what shape I may be in, it is never going to be good enough.

I have heard many women lament that men are interested only in women's bodies, and yet 95 percent of these women's attention is placed on their physicality. This one complains about too much hip; that one, about not enough chest. Another thinks that her legs are too short, and on and on. Somehow we think that if some flaw in our physical appearance could be magically transformed, our lives would be perfect.

A nearly impossible, but necessary, lesson to learn is that we are not our bodies. Yes, if you are reading this, you obviously have a body, but your body is but a tiny speck in the vast sphere of who and what you are. You are first a spiritual being who happens to possess a body. In the Bible it says that a deep sleep fell upon Adam. When we begin to look at life spiritually, we realize that we have all been wandering in a state of deep sleep. As we sleep we dream a collective dream that we are only bodies.

The body is a tiny aspect of who you really are — a glorious and complete being. In this dream, we believe that we *are* bodies rather than that we *have* bodies. Some of us have partially awakened but remain in a sort of twilight state where we have collectively forgotten who we truly are. We continue to play out the scripted dream of being in our body rather than having a body and being so much more than this little speck of tissue, organs, blood, and bones. When we perceive ourselves or others solely as bodies, the ego is the ruler. While we do so, we constantly experience the cruelty of the ego. It is impossible to identify so closely and solely with the body and with others' bodies and not bring pain to ourselves.

As I write today, I am sitting at my table just thirty feet from the beautiful, vast Pacific Ocean. Watching the waves roll to shore, it comes to me that the body is like a wave in the ocean that is God. The ego that sees only the body as a wave cannot fathom the entire ocean.

We must actually train ourselves to give attention to the whole ocean, to get beyond the wave. This begins to happen when we cease judging ourselves or others according to color, size, shape, physical condition, or any other bodily characteristic. This doesn't come easily, but when it is faithfully practiced over time, a new way of perceiving comes into view. I hope the time will come when you can't as clearly define a person's physical characteristics as you can his or her inner essence. You will not notice if a person is of your race or another—I mean, *really not recall*—because you saw into the person rather than gazing at the surface.

Relinquishing judgments is the first step in lifting the barrier of limiting one another to bodies. When we take this step, we can begin to bring the body into alignment with the truth of who we are. The body, yours or anyone else's, cannot contain who you are. The body is a limit on love. At first this suggestion may seem outrageous, but through the years I've had enough experiences to prove that we don't even need the body to truly communicate.

I prayed for a long time before I met my soulmate and husband, David. I prayed to be healed, to forgive, to seek and find the love my heart desired. I meditated on it so much that I was convinced I would recognize him instantly when we met. Through the years I met a lot of men, but none of them felt like I sensed David would "feel."

Then one night while engaged in a complex exercise with a class I was teaching, I suddenly experienced an intense feeling of something remarkable going on that was totally unrelated to the class. I sensed, felt, knew, nearly saw an energy, a presence that was intangible but very real to me. This otherworldly sensation left a permanent imprint in my memory of how the presence of my soulmate felt. I did not feel it again, whatever it was, until about a year later.

I was sitting up in bed meditating early one Saturday morning when I sensed that same presence again. It was gentle and soft, yet powerful, and it seemed to embrace me in warmth and love. It felt wonderful. The whole experience lasted perhaps fifteen minutes, but the afterglow remained with me. I somehow knew I had just met my soulmate. It was not a physical meeting but a spiritual encounter.

In those same moments David had been meditating on meeting his soulmate and extending his field of energy to go forth and find me. It had. I felt it and knew that it was from him, but knew not where he was. What remained with me was a certainty that when we physically met, and I knew we would, we would recognize each other's spiritual essence.

When we did meet in person, David says I gave him what he calls a "Unity hug." In the Unity church of which I am a minister, we are a pretty hugging crowd, and I have developed a way of giving a warm hug without it being sexual or passionate. That, however, was his first physical impression of contact with me. We did instantly recognize each other's spiritual essence, and we laughed because it was our bodies that seemed so unreal. The spiritual essence was what we recognized, were comfortable with, and found to be real.

There is another way to perceive yourself and all others. It begins by experiencing an instant of seeing beyond the body. Then later you glimpse it more frequently, seeing the lovely, seeing through the outer envelope into the inner splendor. You come to know that in the end only this larger sphere is real. Everything else has been but shadowy figures inhabiting our disconnected dreams.

Once we release ourselves from the misperception that we are only bodies, we no longer wish to imprison others in the place from which we have escaped. The obsession with the body is gladly released in favor of the radiance of the inner spirit. The love of God calls us to recognize the spirit in one another and to no longer identify our brothers and sisters as solely their bodies. The attraction of the spirit is irresistible once we have become comfortable enough to let our guard down and explore our depths.

When we see one another as bodies, we have diminished our magnitude and theirs. We have made of love an enemy. We can learn to see the physical world for what it is—a tiny piece of the whole. We can learn to honor, love, find pleasure and delight in our partner's body and still recognize it as a tiny piece of the whole.

The world we see is built on whether we see the physical or the spiritual as the real world. When we choose the physical, we can never escape seeing the body as our reality. When we choose the spiritual, all of heaven bows down to bless us. Then we will see the physical world truly through the eyes of Spirit. In this state we can begin to come into harmony with our true selves. As we individually come into this harmony, we are able to see all of life from this higher point of view, understanding that we are first and foremost spiritual beings having a human experience, rather than human beings who occasionally have a spiritual experience.

A radical shift in how we experience life comes about when we see ourselves, and everyone else, as spirit—a shift no less dramatic than the restoration of sight to a blind person. A way to initiate this shift is to begin gently reminding yourself of your true heritage. This can be done through the use of an affirmation, powerfully repeated throughout the day. One such affirmation comes from *A Course in Miracles:* "I am not a body, I am free, for I am as God created me." Other possibilities are: "I am a spiritual being having a human experience" and "I am spirit." Of course, one of your own will work just as well. These affirmations can be most helpful reminders when we feel ourselves losing touch with our center and getting sucked up into the world and the things of the world.

In recognizing the spirit we naturally move out of living in a helpless victim mode and into a life of mastery. It is impossible to remain a victim when we identify fully with our spiritual nature. As we understand that we are spiritual beings having a human experience, we begin to identify more closely and fully with God, accepting the gifts of God as our birthright. Of course, this transformation in our thinking seldom occurs in a flash. Rather, it evolves and expands over a lifetime of spiritual awakening and soul growth.

People say to me, "Yes, Joan, that sounds great. I wish life was spiritually centered all the time, but it just doesn't work that way in the real world." To which I respond, "The world of spirit is the real world." The world of seeing one another as only bodies, the world filled with feelings of pain and separation and overflowing with dysfunctional behavior, is not the real world. It may be the familiar world, the accepted world, but it is not the real world. Five hundred years ago the fact that most people agreed that the earth was flat did not make it flat. Just because millions of people agree that they and others are no more than bodies does not make it real.

Pain, suffering, sickness, war, and greed are not the *real world*, but they are all "gifts" of the distorted world created by the ego. As we recognize the spirit within us, we begin the process of identifying more and more fully with our true selves.

Mastery is knowing who you are. It is a sense of ease and confidence with yourself and all of life. It is a sense of being in charge, not in a manipulative, controlling way, but of knowing what you are doing, where you are going, and how you are going to get there.

Mastery is being at the helm, feeling empowered and powerful. Moving into mastery, you accept your position as cocreator with God. When you choose to acknowledge the spirituality of self, a new orientation naturally follows, a new way of thinking and being that produces results quite different from the results of the past.

I Thought It Was You—But It Was Me

After realizing the truth that we are primarily spiritual beings having a human experience, the second most powerful, freeing spiritual truth we can comprehend is this: life is really going to work only when each of us takes individual and *total* responsibility for what occurs.

An expression in the Twelve-Step tradition of Alcoholics Anonymous and similar support groups says, "There are no victims, but only volunteers." Grasping that you are not the victim of your life may take a great deal of doing. Just coming to accept the truth of this statement can be incredibly painful. The pain arises out of beginning to release a long-held and false belief system. What we do is cling to these destructive and negative victim thoughts. We grasp so tightly that the clinging becomes a way of life.

Try this exercise. Hold your hand in a tight fist, hard, for thirty seconds. Hold tightly, using all your might. Don't release until a full thirty seconds have passed. Now very slowly begin to let go. As you slowly release your grip, notice how your knuckles feel, your fingers, the wrist and forearm. Be still and experience the sensation of letting go.

Even though you are letting go of nothing, there is still pain because you had clung so tightly for just thirty seconds. Imagine what it must be like to let go of a false concept of self if you have clung to it for ten, twenty, or more years.

The pain of letting go comes from the ego, not from the spirit. The ego goes crazy when it starts to lose its power over us. So the initial stages of letting go can be painful, but what release and relief the letting go soon brings! The spiritually mature take responsibility for their lives. The spiritually immature are always looking for someone to blame.

A great spiritual truth that I have come to understand is that we meet ourselves in everyone we encounter. Two of us could enter the same room, interact with the same people, yet leave the room and report two totally opposite experiences.

To illustrate, I'll use two extreme personalities. Ben and Todd enter a travel agent's office. Ben is coming from his spiritual center, and he's excited about his forthcoming trip. Feeling good about himself and life, he walks in with this light and enthusiasm emanating from him. First he encounters the receptionist, who is on the telephone. She waves and signals that she will be right with him. This is no problem for Ben—he'll just wander over and peruse the travel brochures. In a moment she's free and warmly greets Ben, who proceeds to explain that he's there to buy airline tickets and secure accommodations for his trip. She inquires as to his destination, and he informs her that he's going to Hawaii on business and he's just sure there will be pleasure as well. She is pleased to direct him to a knowledgeable agent who has recently returned from Hawaii.

Ben has a wonderful encounter with the agent, Liz, who is just as enthusiastic as he is. She tells him of a great offer: he can do his business in Honolulu and then stay on an extra week and get free airfare to the neighboring islands. If he will tell her exactly what he wants, she will create a perfect package for him. He will have plenty of time to tend to his business and time to enjoy the aloha spirit. Ben is thrilled and leaves with tickets in hand.

Todd walks into the same agency ten minutes after Ben. He is angry because the parking lot was full and he had to park two blocks away and walk. When he enters the office, the receptionist is again on the telephone with another customer; again she waves and signals that she will be with him shortly. Todd paces back and forth in front of the counter, then assumes a power stance directly in front of the receptionist and begins tapping the counter with his fingertips. She pays no attention to him and continues with the call until it is completed. Todd is fuming by the time the receptionist, in her usual perky manner, asks how she can assist him. He barks at her, "You could have assisted me five minutes ago!" Remaining calm, she asks his destination and he responds that he is going to Hawaii on business. He is told, as was Ben, that Liz has recently returned from the islands and has all the up-to-date information he will need to plan a great trip. Liz is busy with a client at present, however. Would he care to wait for her or see Jack, who is available?

Todd goes to Jack because he has already waited and does not want to waste any more time in this office. He has a very terse encounter with Jack as he states his needs. He collects his tickets and hotel reservations and leaves, deciding not to spend any extra time on the islands. It's a business trip and he can enjoy himself some other time.

Todd leaves believing he was mistreated. Ben leaves feeling great and very pleased with himself for attracting such a great deal. Once again his timing was perfect. Todd is thinking that once again he came out badly on a deal. He feels he was charged too much for his ticket and was booked into a second-rate room. What Ben and Todd experienced at the travel agent's office was a reflection of their individual consciousness. Ben sees the world as supportive and friendly, and his experiences attest to the same. Todd sees the world as confrontational and hostile, and his experiences reflect his view.

Mirror, Mirror, on the Wall . . .

In life we are always encountering ourselves. It is as if everyone we meet is actually a mirror disguised as a person. When I first heard this teaching, I hated it. I mightily resisted it. I thought it was awfully nasty stuff, insanity. In time I've come to know that it is true.

Everyone I encounter is a reflection of my individual consciousness at some level. When, in the distant past, I felt like a victim, there were those who were most willing to fill the role of perpetrator. When I was filled with fear, hurts, and open wounds, all my encounters after the initial politeness would match the energy I was sending out. My negative energy was very carefully concealed behind a mask of niceness that women of my generation had been trained to keep in place. I was very good at pretending that all was well when it was hell.

No one did this to me. I did it to myself each time I denied who I was, each time I settled or said it didn't matter when it did, each time I looked outside myself for my answers rather than within. It wasn't my former husband who needed fixing for my life to be okay. It was I.

This does not mean that I took responsibility for *his* behavior. It is very important that you understand that. It does mean I took responsibility for his behavior showing up in my life. You are not responsible for another person's behavior, but you are responsible for it being in your life. Simply removing yourself from an unpleasant situation is not enough to be healed. To be healed so that we don't go out and create the same old misery again, we must get to the underlying cause and heal it.

Discovering just what the underlying cause may be in your life will take a very high commitment to being healed. To dive into those deep, murky waters is never much fun, but it is always necessary in order to stop re-creating the past over and over again.

Consider for a moment just how many times you have found yourself in the same old situation. You swore it would never again occur, and there it is again. But this time it is worse than before.

When we are still asleep to our spiritual reality, we pretend that we have nothing to do with what shows up in our lives. We're just quietly going along, not causing anyone any difficulty, and this awful stuff just keeps happening. Surely we haven't asked for it, or so we try to convince ourselves and anyone else who will listen. We project what is really our own negative baggage "out there" somewhere, not recognizing it when it boomerangs and hits us in the face. "As hard as I try," we cry out, "why does this same old stuff keep happening to me?" It's happening because of an inner core belief that you deserve to be dumped upon, to be used and thrown away, or whatever your negative baggage may be. You are not at fault, but you are wounded.

Whose-Fault-Is-It? is a favorite game of the ego. Years ago, my first husband and I would bicker constantly. We were both immature children who had no business being married. In our habitual arguing, my spouse would ask, "Whose fault?" It was as if assigning blame in today's argument would make everything dandy. The bone of contention was that I always felt he was finding me at fault, no matter what the argument was about.

From my perspective, of course, I could clearly see that it was his fault, since he wanted to know so badly who to blame. Needless to say, these were not happy times for either of us.

Finding exactly who to blame is not your reason for being here. Healing your psyche, your soul wounds, through forgiveness and love is. Whenever we are tempted to condemn another person, it is because we secretly believe we are only worthy of condemnation. Each time we judge another it is really ourselves that we judge.

James and Tom are both friends of mine. Now James is drop-dead handsome and always dresses straight out of *GQ*. He's very bright, with undergraduate and graduate degrees from Ivy League schools. He's witty, and people are just naturally drawn to him. One weekend we were traveling together to a conference. I had known James for years, but until this trip, just the two of us had never spent very much time together.

Much to my puzzlement, he kept talking about how he could not stand Tom. He scoffed at Tom's appearance, made fun of his taste, his suits, even the kind of sport coats he wore. Tom holds a Ph.D. from a state university and James found fault with that.

It seemed that James loathed everything about Tom. At the time I didn't want to be James's therapist, so I sent blessings to him and Tom and asked the Holy Spirit to heal this dynamic. Then I started thinking, "Does Tom really wear only polyester?" I hadn't noticed. "Stop!" I yelled in my head. "Don't buy into James's grievances and make them your own."

At this conference, James and I were in the same session when the trainer began speaking on the perfect topic. *Whatever we see that we don't like in someone else is a smoke screen attempting to hide what we really loathe in ourselves.* We are terrified to even look at it in ourselves and use our energy to deny it could possibly be in us, when it is so obviously in the other guy.

I was examining how this applied to me when the instructor asked if anyone was struggling with a situation and would like the support of the group to work through it right then. I quickly sat on my hands, lest they betray me and shoot into the air. James spoke up and said he wanted to work through a major grievance he had with a colleague. He began by saying he had been wrestling with his feelings of judgment and disgust with Tom. The instructor asked him to describe what he saw in Tom and to list all the grievances.

The instructor asked James to do a basic technique that I had learned at the very first workshop I ever attended in the early seventies with Ken Keyes, the author of *Handbook to Higher Consciousness.* Here is the technique:

Take a clean sheet of paper and draw a horizontal line across the top. From the center of that line, draw a second line straight down the page.

Now, at the very top center, write the name of a person who has been like sandpaper to your soul, someone who really bugs you. Then put a plus sign on the left and a minus sign on the right. In the plus column write down everything you like and admire about that person, any good you can see.

In one workshop I conducted, a woman wrote only one statement on the plus side: "She writes nice sympathy cards." Now that's stretching, but it will do. Write everything good and when you've exhausted the plus side, move to the minus side and begin to write down everything you cannot stand about that person. It doesn't matter how little or petty it may seem—if you think of it, write it down. Had James been writing down what he was saying, it would have looked something like this:

Tom:

+	−
writes a good presentation	delivers presentations poorly
is good to his children	flirts with women
is punctual	dresses lousy
	looks tacky
	has awful taste
	has no color sense
	wears cheap clothes

Here's the secret. The list isn't about Tom; it's about James. Your list isn't about that other person; it's about you. Sound outrageous, or did you already figure it out?

Here's what James did that really helped him get it. The same technique will assist you as well. Read down the left column of your list and before each item, add the words: "I love myself when I . . . "

Then go to the right column and add the words: "I don't love myself when I . . . "

If you can be brutally honest with yourself, this exercise is a real eye-opener.

Now back to James's list. It went something like this: "I love myself when I write a good presentation. I love myself when I'm good to my children. I love myself when I'm punctual. I don't love myself when I deliver a presentation poorly. I don't love myself when I flirt with women [all the women in the group giggle]. I don't love myself when I dress lousy. I don't love myself when I look tacky. I don't love myself when I have awful taste and no color sense. I don't love myself when I wear cheap clothes."

Now there James stood perfectly coordinated, impeccably groomed and dressed, and all of a sudden he began to shout, "I get it, I get it! Unless I am impeccably dressed, unless everything in the outer is perfect, I feel inadequate, unlovable, undeserving, and unworthy." James concluded, "What really ticked me off about Tom was that he obviously felt just fine about himself no matter how he was dressed or carried himself. I always believed I had to be absolutely perfect just to be acceptable. Even though people told me I was extraordinary, I saw myself as barely adequate. Wow! What a revelation." In those few minutes, James's whole life changed.

I have found this exercise to be incredibly helpful in getting quickly to the underlying issue. Looking at what we cannot stand in someone else, if honestly evaluated, lets us discover what is unhealed in ourselves. Our judgments are never against the other person, but always against ourselves.

A Course in Miracles states, "Everything you behold without is a judgment of what you beheld within." The strain of constant judgment is virtually intolerable. A tremendous release and a deep peace come from meeting yourself and your brothers and sisters totally without judgment. It is but our own self we see when we look upon one another. It is ourselves we judge, condemn, or set free; it is ourselves we love and bless.

Look at yourself, your life, and see what has been in alignment with the spiritual essence of you. Look at what has been partially true and partially clinging to the false, and give that to the Holy Spirit. Be willing to release that which is totally out of accord, turning it all over to the Holy Spirit.

A Course in Miracles speaks of our being willing to give to the Holy Spirit anything that would hurt us. Our false beliefs, judgments, and misappropriations have all hurt us and will continue to do so as long as we cling to them.

We must honestly ask: "Do I want to be rid of this pain? Do I want to be rid of this upset?" If the answer is yes, that yes alone is seldom enough to have the upset and pain vanish. Rather we exclaim, "Yes, I want to be rid of it!" Then, "Now what?"

This is the point at which we are open to help, help from someone who has a more complete grasp of the whole picture than we do in that moment. I am very comfortable identifying that helper as the Holy Spirit, the Spirit of God available to us in a very personal way.

If you feel comfortable with that concept and name, use it. If not, try using "Light," as in, "I release my false and damaging perceptions to the Light." Perhaps you feel a resonance with Divine Love or an angel, or a high being of your religious/spiritual orientation. The name you use is not nearly as important as coming to this vital stage of being willing to release, turn over, or otherwise get rid of what hasn't worked.

If you have been saying for years, "All men are jerks," and all the men you meet appear to you as jerks, then you need to understand that:

1. There are countless men who are not jerks.
2. Your belief is a very negative one to cling to, and it has become a self-fulfilling prophecy.
3. You need more help right now than you are capable of giving to yourself.

This is where you say, "Holy Spirit, please help me get free of this negative belief. Help me be healed, so that I will attract kind, loving, sensitive men into my life. I don't want to live these judgments any more. I now release them to you. Thank you."

❧ 3 ❧

Needy Isn't Attractive

I entered into my earliest intimate relationship as a needy young woman, having fully accepted that I was incomplete without a man. Because of this negative core belief, I failed to see myself as capable of caring for myself, as able to make my own choices, fully express what little sense I had of who I was, or regard myself as complete.

These false beliefs that I clung to as truths caused me to make some very unwise choices, to compromise my values and self. It took me many years, a great deal of pain, and much inner work to finally awaken and value myself above the need to cling to crumbs and attempt to call them love.

Until we awaken spiritually, we go into relationships as extremely needy people, filled with delusional thinking and insane behaviors. If you question the truth of this observation, check out the topics of most TV talk shows on any given day. Or, closer to home, check out the drama playing in your friends' lives—perhaps even in your own life.

Belinda is a lovely woman I have known since she began attending my church a decade or so ago. She kept herself carefully guarded, walled off from me and just about everyone else, never revealing much about herself. There was something mysterious and sad about her. It was as if she carried a great heaviness in her heart, but back then I knew nothing about her personally.

Finally her pain became so acute that she made an appointment to talk with me. As she began to open up, she shared how she had been raised by a mentally disturbed mother and had never known her father, who was of a different race than her mother. Belinda's mother had always rejected her, behaving as if she was ashamed of Belinda's fair coloring and chiseled features.

Growing up in New York City, this beautiful child was constantly ridiculed, beaten, punished, and left alone. While still in high school, she became intimately involved with a man who praised her beauty and artistic talent and promised to take care of her. He offered her a safe haven from her mother's madness and abuse. At age seventeen, she moved in with Carlton.

Belinda was like a starving puppy, lapping up any crumbs thrown in her direction. And that's all she was getting—crumbs. No matter what she did, no matter how much she attempted to please, crumbs were her lot.

A teenaged bride, Belinda was extremely needy in her marriage to Carlton. She needed continual approval and reinforcement that she was okay, beautiful, lovable, bright, and creative. Carlton could not be bothered. He didn't have time for her, was constantly critical, and became easily irritated by her need for attention and approval. After several years of misery with a man who had by then become violent, Belinda—now the young mother of a baby boy—left Carlton. Life had definitely intensified for Belinda.

She moved into other relationships with men who promised to take care of her and her son. The ensuing relationships all resembled her first one with Carlton. She attracted emotionally unavailable men, whom she desperately tried to persuade to fill her empty places. She frantically attempted to get them to love her just as she had futilely sought her mentally ill mother's love.

It took Belinda from age seventeen to age thirty-seven to understand that a man wasn't going to make her pain go away, wasn't going to make everything okay. Belinda was in psychotherapy and spiritual counseling for years. She fully embraced this painful process in order to move through her trauma rather than continue to live out of it. She worked on discovering her core issues so that she could be healed of her soul wounds. Finally she stopped looking for someone or something outside herself to give her a sense of completion and wholeness. She recently turned forty and came to see me to report that she is not only okay but "fabulous!" She now feels unconditional love and acceptance of herself. She has become complete, having learned to fill her own needs. She no longer looks for another, be it mother or lover or son, to do it for her. She has at last learned to love herself and has ceased repeating her original pain-filled relationships.

In her fullness she said to me, "I knew I had to do it, not just for myself, but for my son too. I knew the only way he was going to have a better life was for me to be healed. I couldn't talk about forgiveness and self-acceptance and love without healing my soul trauma. I had to show him by example. It took me so many years to understand that it was my relationship with my emotionally and mentally unavailable mother that I kept repeating again and again in my adult relationships. I did it for myself, and now I can be an example to my son, who is my gift that I love so much."

Is It Love or Is It Need?

The secret grievances we hold onto are the very things we are attracted to in a new relationship. Initially, in our delusional thinking, we call it love.

Here's how it works. While in a state of delusional thinking, we are out of touch with these grievances, for they are living in the subconscious. Since the spiritual principle "like attracts like" is always in operation, that which is held in the subconscious is attracting the same to itself, just as a magnet attracts metal shavings.

When we draw this outer manifestation into our lives, it has a familiarity to it, not because it is of the spirit but because it is of the ego. We have experienced it before, we have attracted it again, and until we are healed of this negative energy, we will continue to attract similar people and circumstances.

Whatever is going on deep within the psyche, whatever we hold to be true—that is *exactly* what we attract. What shows up in our lives in the outer is always a reflection of what is occurring in the more subtle, inner recesses of our minds.

When we come from a place of neediness, it is as if we are unconscious, always looking for our own completion in the outer rather than the inner. Therefore, we draw into our lives not what is truly loving and supportive, but rather another set of circumstances filled with new people and situations that point out to us exactly what still remains to be healed.

Each time we draw into our lives such a new relationship, our hope is that this time it will be different. We are attracted to a new person, and we believe we are in love. But we aren't "new" or clear or healed, so in very short order this fresh relationship, which is still "special," becomes stale. It falls apart, looking very similar to the ones that preceded it.

The bloom of such an unholy or special relationship begins to fade almost at once. All of a sudden, a shift occurs and we cry, "He isn't who he seemed to be at first!" or "She became a spoiled bitch! Who needs her!" Although this ego dynamic is complex, it can be explained in simple terms. In this type of relationship, the ego is the sole ruler. Remember, the ego is that unhealthy part of us that wants to block our happiness at every opportunity. It is an enemy pretending to be a friend.

At this ego-based stage of a relationship, one person's unhealed agenda is attracted momentarily to another person's unhealed agenda. For example, when a man is very wounded he cannot really see his partner; rather, he projects the image he holds of females onto his current partner, who at this stage is a willing party to his drama. This type of relationship is doomed before it even begins, because none of the women he brings into his life will fit his image or agenda for very long. Each will soon demand that he see her for who she is, and this will upset his fragile illusions. These relationships may or may not be broken off at this point, but eventually they will deteriorate.

I know of a couple whose thirty-year marriage operates out of this ego dynamic. The wife holds up her ideal, in which appearances are everything. She runs this motion picture in her head of how romantic her life would be if only her spouse acted a certain way. He would do just those things she saw as best for her. He would say all the right words at the right times. Then her life would be perfect. She doesn't really want a husband—a husband has his own unique personality. She wants a marionette.

The dynamic of the special or unholy relationship is one in which the reality of the partner does not enter at all to spoil the fantasy. In such relationships, the less the other brings to the relationship the better it appears to be for the controlling, needy person. This type of unholy union is an attempt to join with an illusion and then call it "reality," or even "love." It is not reality, it is not love. It is insanity.

Specialness can never be a satisfactory replacement for holiness. Recognizing that we have repeatedly engaged in such ego-based liaisons is the first stage of our own healing. In this initial stage the call for faith is strong, for the relationship may seem disturbed, disjunctive, and even quite distressing. Many relationships have been broken off at this stage and the old unholy pursuits and repetitive patterns taken up again with a new partner in yet another search for specialness. As a minister working with many couples through the years, sadly this is something I've seen happen again and again.

One couple I'll always remember—Eric and Linda—were already married when we met and seemed to have an intense soul connection. I would even say that they were soulmates. They appeared to enjoy each other, have fun together, and have similar interests, including a shared spiritual path. Then a series of events put a strain on their relationship from which it never recovered.

Linda was extremely well educated, holding several advanced degrees. Eric, although bright, had not finished college. Naturally, education was important to Linda, but she said she loved Eric just the way he was, and if he ever wanted to finish college, she would work overtime to support his doing so.

Linda held an upper-management position with a major corporation. She was respected and successful. Eric was in computer sales and was equally successful, although his salary was far less than hers. Then three major changes occurred that rocked their marriage right off its foundation.

1. Linda's company, hit hard by a recession, closed several major departments. Unfortunately, hers was one of them, and she was sandwiched into another department. She was not happy with this arrangement and eventually left. For the first time since graduate school she found herself unemployed.

2. Her father, who had sexually abused her from about age three to age fifteen, contacted her and wanted to make amends and reestablish a relationship. Now Linda had spent years in therapy working on her abuse issues, and although she had moved out of the traumatic energy and memory of it, this was still a major wound she carried. His reappearance tore open that wound.

3. Her preadolescent twin daughters began to go through puberty and act out all over the place. They were outrageously hostile toward their stepfather, blaming him for everything from their declining grades to their emerging pimples. Suddenly they "hated" him and wanted their previous life back with only their mother as a parent. It was quite an awful scene.

Linda, her sense of self-worth challenged on several fronts, began to come apart. The things she had loved about Eric before were all the things she would constantly complain about now. She began to place unrealistic demands on him. She complained bitterly that he wasn't supportive enough emotionally or financially. She didn't like how he was with her daughters, who were regularly throwing raging tantrums. In short, there wasn't much she still did like, let alone love. Sad? Yes. Unusual? No.

With Linda experiencing so many negative challenges in such a short time, she had two choices before her: either project her rising fears and opening wounds onto Eric, or use the reality of what was happening as an opportunity to break through to what could be.

Unfortunately, she chose the first possibility and fled. She could have chosen to step back and review what was occurring as a call to awaken, heal on a deep level, and move more fully into her wholeness. But her inner, traumatized child was nearly frozen in fear. Eric tried to reach her, but she would not allow him in. I called and asked them to come and see me so we could look spiritually at what was going on—that is, discover what was actually happening at the level below all the surface upsets. We talked and I suggested they turn the relationship and all that had recently happened over to the Holy Spirit, asking for spiritual support in order to be healed. We talked about their having a faith and a commitment strong enough to allow themselves to move up to a whole new level of being together and perceiving the light of love in each other for their mutual healing. They both said they would, but soon afterward they separated.

I still feel sadness at their parting, for they are soulmates. Both have a lot to process, forgive, heal, and release, but they really had a spark and that spark has now been extinguished.

What happened with Linda and Eric frequently happens in "special" relationships. Everything appears to be working just as long as no one moves any of the pieces. Within a short time a number of major pieces were yanked out of place for Linda and Eric, and the outer image changed almost overnight. The spiritual essence at Linda's and Eric's cores had not been fully tapped. When there was the opportunity to do so, both ended up in fear and ran. It's sad, but it happens all the time.

At this point the ego encourages us to move into a new, better relationship where the old goal can be better fulfilled, this time with a new person. We substitute a new partner for the old partner with the hope that this one will behave more in accord with our picture.

For several years I have been studying with His Holiness the Dalai Lama. Once, at one of his lectures I attended, someone asked, "What is the purpose of life?" He paused, then thoughtfully responded with his usual broad smile, "To be happy!"

A Course in Miracles teaches that the function of all relationships is "to make happy." Now you and I surely know the majority of relationships we observe do not have as their function "to make happy," any more than most of us understand that the purpose of life is "to be happy."

Our souls are always drawing us toward our joy. It's just that we often aren't ready for it. We don't even know how to recognize or accept it, because we have been so misinformed about the purpose of relationships.

Relationships are not about filling your needs. A needy person is like a human bloodsucker, seeking nourishment, fulfillment, and completion not in himself or herself, but in you. It is a draining, damaging, dysfunctional means of interaction, and it goes on constantly. Linda complained to me that Eric was not fulfilling her needs. Of course he wasn't. That would be impossible for him. He could not heal her insecurities. He could not heal the wounds left by her abusive father, nor quell her raging daughters.

Remember, we cannot be happy in a relationship when we are attempting to force someone else to fill needs that only we can fill, to heal wounds that only we can heal.

When we ask for help through the intervention of the Holy Spirit, we are acknowledging the inappropriateness of our old patterns for our new goal. Until our minds truly accept this new goal as our only goal, the relationship can go through a great deal of strain and conflict. Slower change would not be kinder, however, because dislodging long-established ego patterns requires a radical shift, not a soft, gentle one.

When the healing power of God is invited to be present in the relationship, the old way of interacting is initially threatened and in a very precarious position. It was at this first stage that Linda and Eric bailed out. As time passes, and we remain focused on the possibility of a healed relationship, the old, unholy, special relationship with its newfound goal of holiness begins to be transformed. Judgments begin to drop; demands cease; forgiveness, understanding, and compassion increase. We come to overlook others' mistakes and praise their efforts.

We are able to look within and see the inner beauty there. We are able to look at our partners and see the light shining in their eyes and emanating from their hearts. We are able to feel it within their embrace. The relationship is going through a rebirth, being born anew into holiness. During the birthing stage the call for faith is strong.

We must have faith in the power greater than ourselves to which we have committed the relationship. Faith in the power of the Holy Spirit, which is now in charge of the relationship, will also heal it. When we trust in the power of this love, the job is never half-done. We must also have faith in the innate goodness of our partner and ourselves. Our call for help is always answered, and if our faith remains undaunted, we shall always be guided through the necessary phases of the healing process to completion. We then become free as never before to take our partner's hand and to walk together into love and light and holiness and happiness.

Three Phases of the Healing Process

If you are already in a relationship and the two of you agree to turn it over to the healing power of the Holy Spirit, not all that the relationship contained will be undone or lost. The following guidelines will help you understand how the healing process works and recognize where your relationship is.

1. That which is already truly love and already in complete accord with the purity of your spirit will be retained and lifted up as a blessing to the newly formed relationship.

2. That which is partially in and partially out of accord with the truth of your inner spirit will be separated and the part that is out of alignment drawn from you and released totally. Then the part that is in alignment with truth will be lifted up closer to the Light. For example, when selfless moments are intertwined with selfish ones, the selfless ones will be lifted up and the selfish ones released.

3. Those thoughts, feelings, attitudes, and beliefs that are totally out of accord with spiritual truth will be drawn away from you by your willingness to let them go. These energies are dissipated by the Light of Spirit. They become as impotent causes, no longer able to call forth any effects, which means that the old negative energy will no longer be drawing similar energy and circumstances into your life. When we ask the Holy Spirit to enter our special relationships, we can be assured that Love will respond.

We must be truly willing to let these old, damaging patterns go. In doing so, we are finally assured that the healing has begun and that we can now have a future different from the past.

There will still be times, many of them, when you will be tempted to once again behave insanely: arguing over something insignificant, criticizing your partner, counting her or his short-comings, holding a grudge, misperceiving a hurt, taking something personally that has nothing to do with you—the list could go on and on. If you are honest with yourself, you know how you behave when you are acting out of your ego and not out of the divinely loving part of yourself.

When I find myself caught in such moments, being drawn into an old negative model, I look at myself in a mirror and yell *"Stop it!"* as loudly as I can. This seems to jolt me out of the racing energy of insanity. Then I take a moment and ask that love fill me. Because I am not experiencing peace, I must have gotten off track somewhere. I ask to be shown the way back to love. As we agree to have a complete reversal of the old order and are willing to accept that there really must be a better way, the healing has begun. The way of love, the way that will work, has been accepted.

Although these three phases can occur within an exciting relationship, I have observed them most often as three healing steps within an individual's consciousness and life.

Kim is a live-life-to-the-fullest sort of woman who has experienced phenomenal success in most areas of her life. As a very young adult she achieved great career goals and began making a large income while her peers were still struggling to make ends meet. She oozed brains, beauty, charm, warmth, and style. Others felt good just being around her. By outward appearances she had it all, from her lovely home in the suburbs to her great body.

What Kim didn't have and had never had was a relationship that worked, or at least one that worked for very long. She had been married for nine years and divorced while still in her early thirties. After that she entered into several intense relationships that all followed the same course.

At first they were exciting and romantic. Then the unresolved issues of the past and the history of each partner would arise, the two would struggle for a while, and finally they would sever the relationship. Life for Kim would settle into a routine of socializing with friends until the next Mr. Right rode in on his white charger.

As Kim's spiritual life began to assume more importance for her than her romantic life, she slowly began to heal. In her individual healing work she moved through the three phases outlined above, not in an outer romantic relationship but in her relationship with herself. Initially she recognized that the problem she had with men wasn't out there somewhere. It was "in here," she would say, tapping the center of her chest. From that recognition, she quickly moved through the three stages of the healing process.

First, she reconnected with the knowing that she is a spiritual being, a godded woman, and that all men come into her life to bless her and to be blessed. With this spiritual knowledge grounding her, she could move into stage two, separating the wheat from the chaff. Perhaps you are familiar with the Bible story of harvesting the grain. Mixed in with the good grain, the wheat, is all the other plant life that was growing in the field. That chaff has to be sorted out and discarded. It doesn't belong with the good grain. In our lives this process can be likened to clearing our souls of negativity and living in the rich harvest of love.

Think of the second stage as Kim did—the "threshing phase." The great part about this second step is that we are no longer doing this process alone. One with far more wisdom is leading us. Kim lived in stage two for a while, shifting and sorting, having many breakthroughs—and a few relapses into old behavior. As the depth of her willingness to be healed increased, she began to quickly recognize and release everything that was out of accord with her spiritual love. Here her healing really accelerated.

Now she was ready to move into stage three, which is the point of total release. Stage three is where there is the willingness to let go of everything that has ever hurt us—attitudes, beliefs, thoughts, emotions, memories. Kim was now ready to give to the Holy Spirit *everything* that she held to be valuable or true. Here she recognized that her old beliefs were neither true nor valuable. Her healing has been deep and profound. She is happy, at peace, self-assured.

Kim has dated a few men that she thought perhaps were soulmates, and with whom she felt she could have a holy relationship without conflict and the old ego-based behavior. But she soon clearly knew they were someone else's soulmates, not hers, even though they were terrific men.

Meanwhile, she is enjoying life to the fullest, healed, happy, loving, and free. Is she going to meet and marry her soulmate as she truly desires? You bet! She is ready and tells me she knows she will meet him.

Kim emanates the radiance of one who truly lives out of a consciousness of peace and love. She is at peace with herself and her past. She now focuses on living as a manifestation of love itself, rather than on being in love. Love is in her rather than she in love.

Henri and Rachel are a French-Canadian couple who come from two closely intertwined families. In their growing-up years, family members often joked that these two gorgeous children were going to marry each other and provide them all with exquisite grandchildren. All present would have a good laugh as they nodded in agreement.

For many years Rachel and Henri saw each other more as brother and sister than as potential lover or spouse. In fact, they never had a date with each other until they were both in their midtwenties. As they began dating and their relationship intensified, both families were in ecstasy, particularly when their engagement was announced. The ensuing engagement party was a remarkable affair. I have seen few wedding receptions as elaborate and luxurious as their engagement party.

Henri and Rachel's wedding and their first several years of marriage were like a fairy tale come to life. She personified the princess, and he was her Prince Charming. A disproportionate amount of attention was always given to their physical beauty. It appeared that they were identified by their appearance, individually and as a couple.

Life is about so much more than physical beauty and living in a fairy tale, but neither the couple nor their families understood that.

Rachel worked for an international company and began to travel to France frequently. She would return home from these trips exhilarated. She loved her work, loved shopping in Paris, loved being wined and dined in an opulent style by one of the company's top executives. The evening meetings began quite innocently, or so Rachel thought. In the beginning, upon returning home Rachel would even tell Henri everything about the wonderful times she was having.

On one trip to Paris the executive asked Rachel to stay in France for several more days so they could do some extra work together at his country home. She agreed, told a story to Henri filled with half-truths, and went off with the man who was about to become her lover.

It took eighteen months of more and more extended trips to France, and more and more lies to Henri, for Henri to finally put the pieces together. When he did, all hell broke loose. He was furious when Rachel finally admitted her affair to him. He was devastated and humiliated. He loved Rachel passionately. How could she have done this to them, to their future . . . to him?

Rachel seemed relieved that Henri at last knew the truth, that the lies and the need to always cover herself had stopped. She immediately cut off the relationship with her French lover and begged Henri's forgiveness. But Henri's ego was too bruised. He refused. He wanted nothing from Rachel but a divorce. He said she could have their home, their money, and anything else. All he wanted was *out*. The fairy tale had turned into a tragedy.

Henri was as sad as I have ever known any man to be over a divorce. Rachel cried for two years. She hated herself and seemed incapable of going on with her life. Then, through a series of circumstances, she was led to a spiritual counselor who, after several sessions with her, began to speak to Rachel about the three phases of the healing process.

Rachel had been given just the right teaching at the right moment. She soaked it up like a sponge absorbs water. At first she applied each phase solely to her present self, then to her past with Henri. Rachel began to heal, and then she did a very courageous thing. After not talking to or seeing Henri for nearly three years, she went to his apartment unannounced to see him.

When Henri opened the door and saw Rachel standing there, he was stunned, so stunned in fact that he was unable to move immediately into his stance of anger and unforgiveness. Rachel stood before him a different woman—no longer hurt, guilty, and devastated, but a woman who was whole, healed, and secure within herself. She looked him in the eyes and said gently, "I want to share something remarkable with you over lunch. I'm buying." Taken completely off guard, Henri nodded his assent.

At lunch Rachel shared with him what she had been doing and how she now knew she was healed—healed not only of the frantic aftermath of her affair but also of the underlying causes. Henri listened quietly. He still loved her so. Seeing her once again, he knew that he would always love Rachel.

Then Rachel asked him if he would be willing to do this healing work himself and turn the process over to a power greater than they. She asked if he was willing to be healed of his pain and anger. Henri knew his answer even before she asked the question. Yes, yes, he knew it was time. Henri went to visit Rachel's spiritual counselor and learned about turning his pain and problems and grievances over to the Holy Spirit or Divine Love and what could and would happen if he did.

He moved through the three phases quite rapidly because, I believe, his willingness to be healed was so strong. The first stage was the easiest because he could readily get in touch with his great love for Rachel. He began the process of opening his heart and feeling God's love flowing there. He came to understand that his love for Rachel was a personal expression of an even larger consciousness of love. This love was lifted up and remained as a blessing.

Moving into the second phase took a great deal of sorting, as Henri came to learn which of his beliefs were in alignment with spiritual truth and which were not. He learned to separate the wheat from the chaff within his own life.

Then he was willing to move into the deeper waters of phase three. It was here that he gave up all the rage, self-condemnation, anger, guilt, and ego messages. He worked hard at recognizing that he alone had to do this healing work on himself in order to move on with his life.

As Henri worked at being healed on deeper and deeper levels, he constantly asked the assistance of the Spirit of Love. His requests were consistently answered. After many months of doing this work and experiencing a tremendous release, he said it was as if he had been living in a fog and now the sun was shining brilliantly.

Then Henri asked Rachel to dinner. "It's on me." There he gave her his gratitude for coming to him and sharing what she was learning spiritually. He asked her if she would be willing to begin dating and see where the Holy Spirit led them. Rachel's heart leapt. This was what she had been praying for, if it was to truly be for the highest good of both of them.

It wasn't long until they remarried, this time not out of a fairy tale but out of a deep commitment to their spiritual paths and learning to live in total love.

Spiritual Laws to Live By

As was stated in chapter 2, we are spiritual beings having a human experience and not human beings who occasionally have a spiritual experience. We are Spiritual Beings living in a Spiritual Universe and governed by Spiritual Laws.

We can learn what these spiritual laws or universal principles are and come to align every aspect of our being with them. Spiritual law or principle is that which is unalterable, eternal, not subject to circumstance or humankind's interpretation, and always expressing some aspect of Universal Love. Principle is no respecter of persons. It's like the electricity flowing to your light switch: the electricity does not give you the power to turn on the light because you are either nice to it or crabby with it. It exists whether you choose to recognize it or not. The power is just there, governed by certain laws that, when all is functioning properly, work.

Universal law is always working whether we give it our attention or not. Universal laws do not vacillate; they are changeless. Universal laws are the laws of freedom, and ours are the laws of bondage. Universal laws offer order, love, wholeness, and success to us. Through the individual process of spiritual awakening, we can come to recognize when we are operating out of spiritual laws, which will always be some manifestation of love. We'll also know when we are operating out of the domain of the ego, which will always be some manifestation of fear.

Whenever you are experiencing anything, be it joyful or frightening, ask yourself: "Does this feel like wholeness, order, love, success? Is this a move toward my good?" If your answer is yes, then proceed; if it is no, choose again. When you are confused, ask the Universal Intelligence (which you may call God, Love, Holy Spirit) within you to guide and direct you. As you learn to listen, you will be guided in how to bring your life into alignment with universal laws. It is then that you can experience true joy, the right outworking of situations, a future different from the past. Some universal laws follow.

1. What we focus on expands. To understand totally and live out of this universal law brings remarkable clarity to our lives. Whenever we focus on something within our thoughts, words, attitudes, and emotions, by our very attention to it we cause it instantly to increase, not only in our minds but in our experiences as well.

If you don't want something in your life—an upset with your boyfriend or girlfriend, a mild irritation with your mother—quit thinking about it constantly. Stop repeating stories about what happened. Get rid of the thought that the situation will never change. Release the knot of emotions in your gut.

When you are in any sort of upset, know that it is a choice, and you do have the power to make another choice. You can choose to focus on peace and love and allow these states of being to expand.

2. As we give, we receive. The world perceives giving as costly: once we have given, we have less because we have depleted our storehouse. But from a spiritual perspective, by giving we actually receive even more. To our outer-directed, rational mind this truth is not readily comprehensible. This part of our mind attests that if we have something and we give all or a portion of it away, then we must now have less. That is not what happens in the spiritual act of giving.

Take, for example, the love a mother has for her child. As she gives love to the child, she herself grows in her capacity to love and then has even more, plus she has the joy she receives from just being a part of this new life. In this selfless act of giving, the giver receives even more.

This spiritual principle is at work in every area of life if we allow it to be so for us. The only cost of giving is receiving. Giving something away is how we keep it.

As we give love to one another on this level of understanding, our hearts become pure channels of love and power. The crooked ways are made straight. Our way begins to be lit with miracles. We are opening ourselves to be blessed by miracles drawn to us by the irresistible force of love.

3. *We live in an abundant universe.* Some choose to draw from this abundance, while others deny its existence. As you begin to draw forth from the limitless abundance of the universe, every good and blessing that you desire comes into manifestation.

4. *The power of Love is the only true power.* It is Love that draws to you your own. When I was seeking my soulmate, I wrote this affirmation on several index cards: "Divine Love working through me now draws to me my own." I kept a copy at my bedside and affirmed it once upon awakening and once before retiring in the evening. There were other copies on the refrigerator and on the dashboard of my car. As I repeated this affirmation, I literally felt myself becoming energized by love. I asked the inner spirit to take this energy, this consciousness,

and connect it with the soulmate that I deeply felt was seeking me as I was seeking him.

Another good affirmation to work with is, "The good that I am seeking is now seeking me."

I absolutely possessed a knowing that there was someone who would recognize me as I knew I would recognize him. I already sensed how it would feel to be in his presence. I knew it was just a matter of the right circumstances set into place and we would meet. This was not an illusion, a fantasy, or wishful thinking. It was an absolute knowing, a haunting thought that would not leave me. Our meeting was a certainty, with only the timing being an unknown factor.

5. *Like attracts like.* When we look within and find love, then we are prepared and have the consciousness to attract an outer manifestation of that love. Once you meet and know love within your own soul, you will never be afraid of love again. You will delight in love and behold witnesses to love's presence everywhere. Your consciousness has been transformed; your vibration and intentions are clear.

6. *Our joy is increased through our sharing.* You have to have love first in order to give it away. Love is reaching out. Love offers all things eternally. Hold back from extending love, even in the slightest way, and love is gone. Our function is not to measure who is giving, how much they are giving, or how often they are giving love, thoughtfulness, caring, and so on. Rather, our function is to realize that each time we extend love or thoughtfulness or caring to another, it is a gift not only to the receiver but to us as well. Through our unconditional sharing of love, a multiplying of blessings begins to occur.

As a student of metaphysics for half my life and a teacher and minister for sixteen years, I now know something with such certainty that it can no longer be questioned or debated in

my mind. I know that there are universal laws, or spiritual principles, that govern us and all of life. They exist, are unchange-
able, and always work. I know this as surely as I know the sun is
always shining whether the day is cloudy or clear. We know that
between sunrise and sunset, whether we can see it or not, the
sun is shining. We know if we drop a baseball off a balcony, it is
going to fall downward. It always will. Period. This is the law of
gravity at work.

Spiritual principle works as precisely as the law of gravity.
We just need to get our excess baggage out of the way and move
into the flow so that we can become aware of it. Principle always works. It doesn't like me better than you. I have simply
kept a very high commitment to being faithful to and working
with principle.

If you want love, a holy relationship, to be with your soulmate, then faithfully practice living the principles of love. Work
on yourself and no one else. When you succeed, be ready, because all that will be left is for love to be drawn to you, and
drawn to you in the way that is really best for you.

You can discipline yourself to align your every thought,
word, feeling, and action with the spiritual principle of love. Yes,
the word is *discipline,* which comes from *disciple.* To follow the
path of love is to be a disciple of love, to be a student in training
to master love. To do this, it is necessary to be vigilant for the
truth, to be certain that your thoughts remain in accord with
the spiritual law. When you find your thoughts out of harmony
with love, release the negativity as quickly as possible and bring
yourself back on course. Listen to your words as you speak. Are
they in accord with love? Are they kind, caring, loving, clear,
compassionate, and supportive of yourself and of others?

Feelings take a bit more focus until you become completely attuned to your inner prompters. Are your feelings

light, warm, happy, joyous, and embracing? If not, again release the heavy ones to Divine Love and clear out whatever is still inside that would be pushing love away.

Arnold Patent, a great teacher of spiritual principle, instructs that if we do not have the good we desire, it is because we are pushing it away. Well, when I first heard him say that, I knew it was true but did not fully understand how it was that we pushed our good away. Then it dawned on me that we do this through our negative thoughts, our harsh, angry words, our feelings of unworthiness, our grievances, and all our unhealed "stuff." These block our good and hold love's fulfillment at arm's length. Notice how you are sitting right now. Is your body in a relaxed, open posture, or are you rigid, shut down, and closed off?

Now place your feet flat on the floor, sit up straight, balance your head, relax your shoulders, and open your arms and hands. Take three slow, deep breaths, inhaling through your nose and exhaling through your mouth, and say to yourself, *"Relax."* Notice how different you feel.

This is a much more open and receptive position than the way most people habitually hold their bodies. When we relax and are open, the movement of love in and out can occur without our blocking the flow.

7. *The laws of the universe are the laws of freedom.* The ego's laws are the laws of bondage. Sometimes our ego-mind starts to think that true love, a holy relationship, will never come along. So we try to convince ourselves that "this one" is good enough, that we can compromise, adjust, change him or her just a little, make do, and the relationship will somehow work out.

Before both of my early marriages, there were many warning signs. They clearly said, "This is not right for either of you," but I was oblivious to them. I could not or would not read the proverbial writing on the wall. I forced rather than flowed. I settled for something out of fear of having nothing, and what I got were some mighty intense lessons that forced me to grow through pain. We can grow through pain and suffering, but it is not the preferred way and it is not God's way.

I insisted that my fulfillment had to be found in "special" relationships. You probably have done the same. It does not work. It leaves us empty and bruised, confused and angry. We are angry because what we insisted had to be there was not and could not be there, and thus we are upset and feel let down because of it.

Do not settle for a partner, any partner. Rather than making you happy, it will make both of you miserable. Learn to enjoy your own company. Do for yourself what you have held off doing until you had someone to do it with you or for you. Give up waiting for your happiness to depend on another. Find what gives you joy and do it now. Waiting for someone else to complete you makes you needy, and there is nothing attractive about being needy. It repels all but the dysfunctional people.

Shortly before his death I attended a lecture by the famous columnist Sidney Harris, during which he gave his definition of a "marriage made in heaven." He stated, "A marriage made in heaven is where the holes in her head fit perfectly with the rocks in his." That is a great definition of a special, needy relationship.

You are free to move into such a relationship, or you can choose to be really good to yourself and read the handwriting on the wall, thereby saving yourself years of anguish. I have noticed through the years that what at the beginning of a relationship people insist really doesn't matter is exactly what does matter a great deal after the initial glow begins to fade. Life can be heaven. Why do we insist on making it hell?

8. *The laws of the universe are always cause and never effect.* When you can keep your focus solely on the cause and give no

attention to effects, you are then aligning yourself with the divine and entering into the universe's higher order of being.

Spiritual principle unfailingly works, but you have to be ever faithful. Do not put your faith in the ego's ways; place all your faith in spiritual laws and know that you are not allying yourself with the shifting and changing but with the eternal. Your faith removes all limitations and obstacles. There is no problem that faith and unwavering commitment will not solve. This principle of faith truly can move mountains and will bless your life with unimaginable good.

There will be times when you are tempted to give up, to return to your former ways of living, judging, and alienating. These times are when the need for faith is greatest. Call upon the Holy Spirit, who comes by invitation, and ask that your tiniest piece of faith, which you now give, be magnified until it is powerful enough to see you through your difficulty.

This is what is meant by needing a "grain of mustard seed" portion of faith. If you give just the smallest amount, the universe will multiply it until it becomes the full portion necessary. Don't give up. Remember the words of Richard Bach in *Illusions,* "You are never given a wish without also being given the opportunity to make it true. You may have to work for it, however." And you may have to work for it for a long time.

I am reminded of the acquaintance who said he didn't know if he should go back and complete college at age forty-three. If he did, he would be nearly fifty by the time he graduated. I asked him, "How old will you be in seven years if you don't go back to school?"

If you hold within your heart the dream of a holy relationship, and you hold within your heart the knowing that love can be profound and easy, without conflict and struggle, you are on the right track. Just because you are on the right track doesn't necessarily mean you've arrived at the station, but it does mean the journey has begun. So if you are 100 percent committed to your journey, you can just enjoy the trip, knowing that you will eventually arrive at your destination.

In the last years of his life, Winston Churchill returned to the boarding school of his youth to address the assembled body of young boys. Mr. Churchill was quite feeble at this stage of his life. He quietly sat on the dais waiting his turn to speak. When introduced, the prime minister, the respected world leader who had risen out of these roots, slowly made his way to the podium. Steadying himself as he rested on his cane, he looked out upon a sea of shining young faces filled with hope and the promise of unlimited opportunities. He faced these bright boys with their expectant, excited eyes and stated simply, "Never give up, never, never, never, never, never give up." And he slowly turned and methodically made his way back to his chair.

Never give up. A grand lesson. Principle will always work. It is the law. It is universal law. It will work. If it has not worked and you are impatient, you must realize that there is a reason. The timing is not right, and something still needs to be brought into place. This is where you need faith, but never give up, never, never, never. Principle always works.

⊠ 5 ⊠

Look Through Loving Eyes

The Golden Rule states, "Do unto others as you would have them do unto you." Such clear and simple words—you would think we could easily understand and live by this message. Sadly, this generally is not the case. Many folks go through life with a scorecard. They keep records of who did what, when, how often, how expensively, how appropriately, and to whom. Tallying up every act and gesture in an attempt to ensure that life is always fair just doesn't work. If you must count, count your partner's or potential partner's attributes and not the flaws.

To see the lovely we must lighten up. This will take some practice in a society that programs us with ceaseless reports of negative events. The daily newspapers and the nightly news primarily report disasters and dastardly deeds. What we seldom hear are stories about the countless people who were not robbed, raped, or riddled with bullets.

I've noticed that the news programs are attempting to lighten up. Now they're showing the regular twenty-six minutes of horror followed by a thirty-second filler of good news. Thirty seconds of something positive is hardly enough to turn the tide. Recently, on a chilly late-October morning, I officiated at a wedding held in the Cleveland Stadium. The bride and groom were major Browns fans, and their wedding made the news of the local NBC affiliate. This brief upbeat segment was supposed to air at noon, six, and eleven. It seems too many reports on that day's misery had to be covered, however, so by the eleven o'clock broadcast, the thirty-second positive conclusion had been dropped.

I'm from Cleveland, a city with far more to offer than stand-up comics would have you believe. Now our reports of crime and drugs and terror probably equal those found in any major market. Recently a local TV newsman who is a member of our church asked a group of us, "Just how many murders would you guess occurred in downtown Cleveland last year?" One person said, "Three hundred and sixty-five. By the news reports, about one a day sounds right." Another said one hundred; another, twenty. The answer was one, a drug-related conflict . . . *one!* The news is presented in such a terrifying way that many suburbanites are terrified of nonexistent villains and won't venture into town.

We are bombarded with negative reports. We are constantly seeing and hearing about the sleaziest side of human existence. The focus is continually on the blood and guts, on what will boost the ratings. This mass of negativity pollutes our collective consciousness, clouding our ability to perceive accurately what is really happening. Isn't it curious that we call this daily telling and retelling of every negative event the "news"? I think it could more accurately be called the "olds," since it is always the same old thing.

If you fill your head with the news and the standard talk-show fare of who is doing what atrocity to whom, if you watch the stories of "special" relationships that unfold on the soaps, then it will seem like an impossible task to seek and find the lovely.

In the Dhammapada, a fifth-century-B.C. scripture, we read, "All that we are is the result of what we have thought." If all day long you are hearing nothing but garbage, at the end of the day your head will be filled with nothing but garbage. We must turn off the exterior input of ego battling ego in one form or another and begin to cleanse our consciousness. It is impossible to see only the lovely if our input has been only the ugly. This does not mean that you should become an ostrich and bury your head in the sand, but it does mean that you must put the negativity of the world's reports into proper perspective.

Seeking the lovely means looking past outer appearances into the inner core of the people involved and finding beauty there. It requires looking beyond what someone has chosen to do with circumstances and conditions to what is inside. If you look deeply enough and long enough, you will find beauty. You *will* find beauty.

People have scoffed at this idea and said, "You don't know my ex-spouse." I've responded, "No, but I know God." If you are like one of these people, what I'd like for you to do is think of that former spouse, former lover, or whomever you are holding grievances against. Now see that person not as he or she is today or was when you were together. Instead, go back to when the person was a teenager, a child of ten, a seven-year-old, a five-year-old, a toddler, a tiny baby. See that man or woman now as a tiny newborn infant. See him or her innocent, fresh, and pure, looking out at life with wide-eyed wonder.

Now, still holding that image, do the same for yourself. Take the thought of yourself back through your teen years to preadolescence, to when you were seven, five, two years old, to when you were an innocent infant. See the beautiful child you once were. Love that precious little one. See her perfection. See his perfection. A lot has happened since you were that perfect child. The same is true of your former spouse or current significant other. It is true for each of us.

At one time, all we knew of ourselves and of the world was the innocent. Then a great deal occurred in our lives to obscure that innocent beauty. I recently met a woman who described this natal innocence as all of us being born with a pure white soul. Then each time we experience hurt, each time we feel unloved or unlovable, it's as if a dark smear has been rubbed across the whiteness. This marring of the soul continues with each separating act until many lose sight of that innate inner purity. Just because all that "stuff" happened does not make it true. It is not our reality unless we choose to see it as such.

The innocent awareness that we all had at some time is our spiritual truth. Although it has been obscured by piled-up layers of defenses, hurts, and ugliness, that purity remains at the center still emitting its light. It is the innocent one in us that can perceive truly. When we come from that pure place within us, we can see what was originally created and not just the mess we have made of it. Don't remain a prisoner to the false image. You can learn to see through it to the pure, innocent divine child who patiently awaits your recognition.

When I was in training for the ministry, one of our weekly assignments was to spend half a day each week at a nearby county hospital. I was to spend this time visiting the patients, praying with them, and simply loving them. Most of the patients were wards of the state, without family or resources. It was a fairly grim place. Besides being sick, the patients were depressed and lonely and had an aura of hopelessness about them. It was a pretty dismal experience for me initially. It was something I had to do as a class assignment, and I didn't know how I could do it. In the first several encounters there, I felt like a miserable failure. My chin would begin to quiver, I would get nauseated and start to cry just walking into the place. Great, I would think, how can I ever become a minister and tend to sick people when all I can do is stand before them and blubber? It was awful. I was a mess, having to do it and not being able to do it.

When I shared my conflict with a friend, she sat, listened intently, then thought for a moment and said, "Don't focus on their conditions or their rambling words. Simply look into their eyes. See into their souls through their eyes. See the divine in their eyes. See their divine self looking back at you. See their innocent, pure, happy child and bless them as God would have you do." That was a turning point in my ability to minister to those people and all the people that would follow.

We can all learn to look within, past the outer appearances to the inner divinity, to the innocent infant. When you look at those you profess to love, look not at what they have chosen to make of themselves in these moments, but at what was originally created.

Go to the mirror, strip down to your birthday suit, and look through the body into your essence. See into your eyes until you behold that little newborn baby filled with purity and awe and infinite possibilities for good. The attraction of guilt has become powerful in this world: we condemn first ourselves and then everyone else in our path. Let your mistakes drop away. Let your lover's or spouse's mistakes drop away. Set that person free from guilt and allow him or her to be revealed to you as the wholly lovable person that he or she is.

Every moment, we choose whether to look at the flaws or to look at the lovely. Focus gently upon your friend and you will find much that is lovable. What we focus on expands. Focus on what you perceive as lacking and that seeming lack grows and grows, becoming all you are capable of seeing. The day comes when you can see nothing else because you want nothing else. Whatever we see is a reflection of our own consciousness. What we see isn't necessarily real, but it is what we want. Do you want to see your lover's innocence or your lover's guilt? Your decision does determine what you see, and whatever you decide to see in your friend is exactly what you have decided the verdict is to be for yourself as well. See him as guilty—you see yourself as guilty. See her as innocent—you see yourself as innocent. Whatever you see without is a judgment of what you see within. *A Course in Miracles* teaches not that we should not judge, but that we are incapable of judging; we are too filled with our own unresolved conflicts to be able to judge. It teaches that when we think we are judging another, it is as if we hold above that person's head a sword suspended from a thin cord, but when the sword falls, it is upon our own head. It is always ourselves we are judging. If we could remember this, we would become much more charitable in our perception of one another.

Our inner spirit holds out to us the real world as it was intended to be. We can choose to make the glad exchange for it, relinquishing the harsh, cruel world that we have created. This idea is summed up in these words from *A Course in Miracles:* "As you look upon [this new world] you will remember that it was always so." Choose to see the sweetness in life. It can be found in every situation when we are open to seeing it.

Be content no longer with littleness. Become willing to see yourself and everyone else as they were originally created: holy, innocent, pure, lovely, and lovable. Focus on the beautiful and it will expand.

What a world we will have when we see only the purity that is in each of us. Our world will be lit by miracles.

Love: A New Definition

The kind of love I'm talking about is not the love that is commonly perceived. It is not sentimentality; it is not trying to find someone to fill your emptiness or needs. The kind of love I am speaking of is not what is commonly held as realistic in popular psychology. It is not about give-and-take, or sacrifice, or compromise.

The kind of love we are exploring is divine. It is of God, it is guarded by heaven, and it bathes your spirit and soul in light, peace, and joy.

This kind of love allows you to relax and stop looking over your shoulder. It is coming into holy union with the divine and then bringing that holiness forward to bless your life, your relationship, and everyone you encounter.

There are a few things in life that I truly know, and one of them is that we are here to love one another. The great spiritual teachers have all taught, "Love one another." Simple, yes. Easy? Not until we really get into the wonder of life.

Our world so easily becomes choked with the meaningless and insignificant. Our thinking has gotten so upside down, it's as if we've been pulled into a black hole of madness, greed, and hate. All the while, the inner spirit is calling us to awaken and be joyous. Our goal is to find delight in the everyday wonders of life and see the miracles that are everywhere.

One morning, while on retreat in Molokai, I arose before dawn to meditate as I do every morning. I was in the midst of a deep meditative experience when I got an inner prompting to open my eyes. There before me was the most magnificent predawn wonder: a view of the sea and sky and distant islands I had never imagined possible. The whole world, as far as my eyes could see, was awash in countless shades of lavender—a lavender sea, lavender sky, lavender mountains, lavender clouds, all framing Maui and Lanai. It filled me with awe and I felt the presence of love washing over us all . . . not just me, but you too, all of us. In this mystical moment I felt embraced by the miracles of life and could see the wonder of it all. It was a moment, a holy instant, when I truly understood how blessed I am, how blessed we all are when we just open our eyes to see and our hearts to feel. It is then that we know how loved we are.

While stuck in our ego-mind we attempt to ignore, deny, or disregard this sacred, knowing part of ourselves. This part can bring us true and eternal fulfillment and satisfaction. All it takes is one holy instant of grasping the wonder of it all, and we can come to know love as it was created. We will no longer be attached to the sickly image we have made of it. Rarely do most of us live our lives as if we knew this to be so, either for ourselves or for anyone else. How many of us have attempted to keep doing, achieving, acquiring, and yet remain unfulfilled, empty on the inside?

Ken was a good-looking, graying-at-the-temples sort of guy. He had just passed forty and had never been in a fulfilling relationship. His pattern was that he dated and rejected one available woman after another. In desperation he came to see me. All of a sudden he was feeling less virile, tired, hollow, broken, and old.

He had just bought an older home that needed major renovation, but he no longer had the desire or commitment to finish it. So what did he do? He went out and bought a new BMW convertible and a new wardrobe. These bolstered his sense of virility for about ten days, and then once again he felt empty. Nearly every weekend he was with a different woman. None of the relationships lasted. His life had become one unfulfilling acquisition after another of things and relationships.

Ken finally became fed up with his superficial, totally outer-directed lifestyle. Even his closest friends had grown weary of his recurring drama. The situation became unbearable. One of his friends "threatened" Ken with never accepting another of his phone calls until he came to see me and looked at his life and his unsuccessful search for love.

Ken was really no different from many other people of my generation. He was searching for acceptance and love in places and things where it is never to be found. Material possessions can be enjoyable and fun, but they can't, as the Beatles sang when I was a teenager, "buy me love."

Ken made the decision to stop dating altogether. Through counseling he understood that, just beneath the surface, he was living as a frightened, abandoned boy of four. This little Ken had experienced the death of his mother when he was at that tender age. Distraught, Ken's father went into a deep depression and had to be institutionalized for a while.

Ken recalled how, at that time, he made a decision that for decades was the core belief from which he lived. He decided that he could never rely on or trust an adult. The only one who would ever be there for him was himself. Understand that this was a four-year-old child thinking in this manner. Consequently, he simply wouldn't trust any adult, male or female.

At four years of age Ken had to make such a decision for his own emotional survival. At forty, that decision and its negative effects did not serve him at all.

Learning to look within and begin his healing process was terrifying for Ken. But his commitment to changing his life was strong enough to drive him to do the inner work he had to do. Through this work he learned to love and care for his abandoned four-year-old, to reclaim that child and allow him to be a little boy, to be tended to, cared for, and loved.

Then, as Ken put it, "I began to grow up for the first time." Ken's life and lifestyle have come to a place of centeredness. He's comfortable with himself, no longer consuming and running, and he is content with his life. For now he remains a bachelor—a peaceful and happy one—and for the first time in his life he is ready for a fulfilling relationship.

Money can buy many things and we may even derive pleasure from these things, but money never could and never will buy true love. Nothing in the outer can give us a lasting sense of value. We can spend a lifetime searching in the outer world for fulfillment, accomplishment, or worth and all the while the greatest treasure has been locked within our hearts.

This presence within you is ever calling, beckoning you to return to your true self, to pursue goals that are worthy of such a noble one.

If there's an old fear that says, "You'll have to do without," instantly turn it over to the Love within you. This doesn't mean you will have to do without, but it does mean you will have to get used to doing without that old negative belief, and that you will be accepting a whole lot more good into your thoughts and life. Love is a spiritual Presence and Power. It is an energy that anyone can feel. Even our pets can sense those who would love them and those who would do them harm.

For over sixteen years I was guardian to Shannon, a six-pound Yorkshire terrier that was a manifestation of unconditional love and total acceptance. She was, as Jean Houston used to say about such endearing animals, a "bodhisattva pet." In Buddhism, a bodhisattva is a manifestation of the Buddha that is pure love, compassion, and acceptance.

Maybe once in a lifetime, if you are very blessed, a bodhisattva pet will come to live with you. These are the animals that seem to be wiser than most of the people you know. They're the ones that don't just look at you but appear to be looking into your soul. With this type of pet, communication without words is the norm.

This type of pet just loves, has no problem with commitment, is loyal, and seems to know intuitively when you are hurting. In all the years I had Shannon, she was a total manifestation of unconditional love. Her life's mission was to love. I would kiddingly say that she was my "child substitute." Since I was never able to have children, she was like a precious, adorable, loving child to me.

She had a radar that was uncannily accurate. Shannon loved nearly everyone. Once, though, I had neighbors in the adjoining condo who, I later learned, were suspected of being white-collar drug dealers. If we were outside or in the hall when their "company" came, Shannon would shy away from these neighbors and all their "guests." If she was leery of someone, I learned to be also.

It may sound strange, but having such a treasure as my pet for sixteen years taught me a lot about unconditional love. Her love was so huge that it could fill a room and often did. It filled my heart when she was with me, and even now to think of her after she's been gone for eight years. As I say in wedding ceremonies, love never dies, love never ends. Love is an energy that entirely fills the heart. Its warmth melts the walls of ice or crumbles the walls of cement that we have erected out of pain, hurt, or fear. Love is a healing balm. It is a warm, soft, gentle, smooth, tranquil field of being.

Seek for the Barriers

Our task is not to seek for love, but to find all the barriers we have built against it. In our wounded state, unhealed of past and present pain, we have locked up our true essence in a prison of our own making. Each block in our encampment is made out of a fear, a sense of abandonment or separation. Our all-powerful minds have built this enormous prison, locked our vulnerability, innocence, and love inside, and thrown away the key.

Noel kept searching outside herself and her relationship with Tony for what was missing. Despite years of searching in new relationships, a new career, even a new identity—she chose a "new" name—she never found what she was looking for until she stopped looking outside herself and began to look within. There she found what she believed had been missing in her marriage with Tony. She began to discover Noel, acknowledge herself, and love herself. Says Noel: "For twenty years my energy went out trying to change Tony, not accepting him. I was exhausted, depleted of energy. After so much work on myself I finally had a healing and felt a burst of compassion, tenderness, and caring. It was like, all of a sudden, everything that had been an issue was no longer an issue." She could then, for the first time in their twenty-year marriage, look at Tony and see the beautiful, faithful, kind, loving soul that this man is and had always been.

While Noel searched for magic and a soulmate, Tony willingly gave her the space she needed to "find herself." He loved her from afar as, on his own, he raised their two daughters and kept the household going.

After nearly three years of struggling and searching, Noel did find her soulmate. He was at home taking care of their kids. Sometimes that which we seek is right in front of us. It is at the kitchen table or beside us in bed, but we are so filled with our own unhealed stuff that we can't see the treasure in our own backyard.

Your soulmate may be in the next room, but if you have been projecting your unhealed agenda upon him, it becomes really difficult to see his light. You may be unable to recognize who she really is and to appreciate her worth.

So often we mistakenly believe that our worth is determined by our accomplishments, by what we do or what we possess. Ken and Noel and countless others have fallen into that trap. The truth is, nothing we do or accomplish establishes our worth. Our worth is established by God. Noel was searching for her sense of worth outside herself. For a very long time she sought fulfillment in empty places, never finding the happiness she was seeking until she awakened and began to value herself and what she had all along.

I gave a dear friend, also named Joan, a little printed sign that reads, "If you want to be one of the chosen, choose yourself." Until we can make that choice, we are no good to ourselves and ultimately no good to anyone else.

When Noel was finally able to make that choice, her life began to turn around. It was then that she could see the treasure that had been waiting in her own backyard.

The Dream

Nineteen eighty-four was a very challenging, painful year for me. Everything was such a struggle then; nothing was coming easily. I had just gone through a hurtful and miserable second divorce. I felt fragile, old, unwanted, and insecure. As if life was not intense enough, I then resigned my position as minister from my first church and was about to begin a brand-new church with a handful of people. I was traumatized by my experience and filled with fear. I began having anxiety attacks.

My whole world seemed to be crumbling—and it was. At the time, I thought I had to be very strong and powerful just to survive. I couldn't let anyone know how terrified I was, how fragile my facade had become.

Then one night just before leaving to go on a weeklong retreat in California, I had this dream:

I found myself inside a large, beautifully restored Victorian mansion. I was in the house by myself walking from room to room, admiring the craftsmanship and furnishings, when I came into a hall with a large exterior window. I stopped and looked out this window, and from this vantage point I could see the front door of the house. On either side of the front door were full-length windows.

I found myself looking out this hallway window toward the front door, where I was able to see back into the house through the glass side panels. What I saw was a beautiful, soft, feminine young woman, filled with wide-eyed wonderment, slowly descending an elaborately carved wooden staircase. She had already reached the upper landing. In the dream I absolutely panicked. I started shouting, "No! No!" and raced in sheer terror through the house to the staircase. Reaching the bottom of the stairs and looking up, I saw before me this serene, silent, luminously beautiful woman. She looked down on me with wide-eyed wonder and with total love and compassion. And I screamed in terror: "Who told you that you could come out? You must go back! You can never come out. It is not safe for you. Go back, go back, before it's too late!"

It was too late. The proverbial cat was out of the bag. The beautiful spirit was out of her attic prison.

I left for California the next morning with the image of that woman in the dream haunting me. I searched for a figurine that resembled her, with soft, chestnut, shoulder-length hair and a flowing willow-green-and-white gown. She was so innocent, so vulnerable, so pure, and so divine. She simultaneously terrified and fascinated me. I knew she was an archetypical image of me, and all I wanted to do was ignore her. But she would not go away. My panic subsided just long enough for me to ask my inner spirit to reveal what her message was and why she had come out on her own.

She was I. I was she. She was that part of me that was pure love, which I had kept locked away, cloistered behind years of unresolved conflicts, old grievances, hurts, anger, guilt, and fear. Slowly at first, I began to peel away those defensive layers. It was like peeling the layers of an onion, and like the onion, it brought a lot of tears. Then came release, and the realization that she had been with me always, through my early marriages, through all my struggles. It truly was time to let her out. It was time to let out the love that I had so carefully protected and locked deep within my soul. The beautiful spirit was released from the attic.

In that year and in all the years since, I have taught, learned, and practiced how to remove love's blocks and release what Robert Browning called the "imprisoned splendor." Before this awakening, I, like most of us, held a fantasy, an illusion, of what love was or was supposed to be, and I was always disappointed. The illusion of love could never satisfy, but only after I began to awaken to love's presence could I discover its reality, which offers everything. Until then, it was as if I was asleep to love's gifts. When we sleep, the love inside us remains ever awake and vigilant in its desire to gently awaken us. As soon as we make the weakest of requests, love will enter our mind and begin to heal us. The healing that love brings is always gentle. Love does not conquer all things, but it does gently transform all things.

Our egos are so crazy that they are forever thinking in terms of conquest, but love does not do battle, does not conquer. Battle is the sole domain of the ego. Love is like soft water gently healing our wounds.

6

Examine Your Patterns

In traveling my own spiritual path, I did not really start to wake up until I left my second husband. At that point, my pain was so intense that I knew I had to get to the core, or life was not worth living. I was willing to do anything, go anywhere, as long as I felt guided onto that path.

I trekked to India with two companions.

I went through the rebirthing process a number of times.

I saw several counselors.

I wrote forgiveness lists for thirty minutes a day for years.

I asked the Holy Spirit to shift my perception and heal my pain.

I released and released and released.

I kept a journal.

I attended Dr. Jean Houston's Mystery School in New York State for two years.

I studied *A Course in Miracles* for years, doing a daily lesson that focused on holy relationships.

I Master Minded with prayer partners.

I prayed and meditated daily.

I participated in numerous self-growth and healing workshops and retreats.

I looked at my negative, self-defeating patterns and fields of energy, which perhaps had been in place for a lifetime, and I asked to be changed in my depths.

I affirmed and affirmed and affirmed, visualizing myself happy, healthy, wealthy, healed, and free.

I was committed and I knew what I wanted. I wanted to be healed of the past, distant and recent. I wanted to live in a committed partnership with my soulmate in a holy relationship. And I knew that God always says yes when we are clear on what we want.

I was ready. Life had tempered me. I asked for a future different from the past. I quit dating and went to work on myself as one driven by life's passions. It was my fervent desire to be healed of such insanity and be ready for my soulmate. I knew he was, as the song goes, "somewhere out there . . . " and I was getting ready.

What I came to understand is that spiritual laws or principles are available to us as a guide and code by which to live our lives. When we awaken to and follow these principles, all aspects of our lives come into harmony and order. When we live out of accord with these spiritual principles, we wreak havoc on our lives, which become unimaginably messy. Remember that spiritual principle always works when you practice it. Spiritual law is not up for debate; it is not something that works sometimes and is on vacation at other times. It always, unfailingly, works!

Another example of a spiritual principle is: Love is our reality. We don't have to create love. We just have to discover and remove the blocks or boulders that obscure the light of love.

My motivation was as high as it could be. I knew it was necessary to recognize my problems and heal them. I was not the problem, but my old hurts, traumas, pain, fears, mistakes, and judgments were the problem. I had come to realize that the ego does not directly say you did something wrong. It states that *you* are wrong.

If you have examined your life at all, you most likely are already aware of some areas that need correction. Now I'm not talking about, "I just need to get rid of all these bastards around me and my life will be perfect." If you perceive your life as filled with bastards, then you need to realize that they are residing in your life at your (probably subconscious) request, to assist you in waking up.

When you actually wake up is entirely in your hands. You can do it now, or you are free to add more years of living in ego domination to your existence. We don't wake up until we are ready.

One Sunday morning in Molokai, Hawaii, I attended a lovely service in a simple chapel across from a massive expanse of turquoise and sapphire sea. It was Valentine's Day, and the minister, in place of a sermon, had arranged to honor the elder wahine (women) members by having five of them share their hearts' messages of love and faith. It was so precious to see each sweet, inexperienced speaker move past her shyness and speak her heart's message.

One dear woman, Auntie Louise, who was perhaps eighty years old, said she had not awakened until three and a half years ago. Some in the congregation giggled, but I understood perfectly what this wonderful Hawaiian grandmother meant.

You may awaken now, or when you are eighty-five, or at the moment of death. Perhaps you are already in the process.

Once we set the course, there can be no turning back. We may experience delays and setbacks, but once we have placed our feet on the path of healing, we can never go back to what or who we were.

The Iceberg

All of us, on one level, are aware that we have issues and memories that need to be healed. But the awareness that there is a problem is like the tip of an iceberg dwelling on the surface of our minds, while beneath the surface is a mother lode of which we are unaware. It is a mother lode of unhealed, unprocessed, deeply buried hurts, regrets, anger, resentments, and fears out of the past. Unfortunately, no one seems to be exempt from the need to do this inner healing work.

Approximately one-tenth of the mass of an iceberg can be seen above the surface, while the other nine-tenths lies beneath the surface. This is an apt image for our lives, because one-tenth of what we know we have to work on is right out there for us to see. We need to clear up this surface stuff, but the shocking news is that it's only one-tenth; the remaining nine-tenths has been carefully hidden by our ego. It is disguised and denied, but it hasn't gone away on its own, and it can't go away without intensive work. That is why, when you really get down there into it, you may discover bits and pieces of negative energy wrapped around your soul. They may have been buried there years and years ago, but just because it is old does not mean it has ceased to wreak havoc in your life.

We need to recognize the problem so that it can be healed. This is not about living out of the energy from that old hurt or pain or experience. It is about recognizing it for what it is: a field of negative energy that fits perfectly into a life pattern that you no longer want!

One young woman I worked with years ago was extremely committed to her own healing. Audrey had been in therapy for four years and it had been helpful, but she was still feeling exposed and raw. As we talked, she recalled how her parents had divorced when she was four; she spoke of her last memory of her father being some very traumatic moments as he drove away with all his earthly possessions. She was still feeling the pain thirty years later as she retold her story of a sobbing little girl crying, "Please don't leave me, Daddy; please don't divorce me, Daddy! I'll be a good girl!" She never saw or heard from her father again.

She carried a soul wound that announced to all potential partners, "Men leave me." So she found herself attracted to dapper Don Juan types who were just like her father, only a generation younger. They would love her and leave her, no matter how hard she cried and promised to do more, to be more, to be in essence the "good girl" of her wounded four-year-old self.

She had carried for three decades the energy and hurt of her father's leaving, and she kept reliving the experience again and again as an adult. Once she understood what had been happening, she could begin to do the healing work necessary to resolve the conflict, heal the wound, and create a future different from her past.

Let's examine the iceberg imagery in more detail, using Audrey's story. On the surface of Audrey's life, she was aware that her father's leaving must have wounded her. She also knew

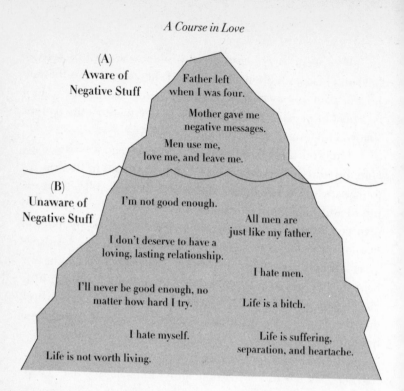

(A)
Aware of Negative Stuff

Father left when I was four.

Mother gave me negative messages.

Men use me, love me, and leave me.

(B)
Unaware of Negative Stuff

I'm not good enough.

All men are just like my father.

I don't deserve to have a loving, lasting relationship.

I hate men.

I'll never be good enough, no matter how hard I try.

Life is a bitch.

I hate myself.

Life is suffering, separation, and heartache.

Life is not worth living.

that her mother had given her many negative messages about men in general. Recently she had become aware of the repetitive negative patterns in her intimate relationships. These awarenesses go into the top one-tenth of the iceberg (*A*) under the heading, "Aware of Negative Stuff."

At this point Audrey was just beginning to realize that much was hidden in the bottom nine-tenths, "Unaware of Negative Stuff." Through sustained counseling, processing, and inner work, she gradually could uncover the long-held negative beliefs buried beneath the surface (*B*).

This witty, charming woman did not consciously know she carried so much internal garbage. She just knew that she had experienced nearly constant pain and that her life was miserable and unmanageable.

I suggested that she begin with a technique for bringing up from her depths that old, stagnant, solidified energy. One of the most effective ways of doing this is to create an affirmation, a positive statement of spiritual truth that may be the exact opposite of what one is experiencing in the present moment.

Audrey took her statement found in *A*, "Men use me, love me, and leave me," and turned it into an affirmation that stated what is spiritually true, "Men always want the best for me." This affirmation was the exact opposite of the negative core belief of her wounded self, which constantly gave Audrey the message that "Men only care about themselves." She was instructed to write this affirmation thirty times a day, and after she wrote the affirmation to write down any negative response that came into her mind.

Her writing went like this:

Day 1

Men always want the best for me.
Ha, that's a laugh.

Men always want the best for me.
Where are these men? I haven't met any.

Men always want the best for me.
Bull!

Men always want the best for me.
Men want the best for themselves.

Men always want the best for me.
Men can only think of themselves.

Men always want the best for me.

Men are all selfish bastards like my father.

Men always want the best for me.

They love you and leave you. Who needs them?

Men always want the best for me.

I hate my father for leaving my mother and me. How could he do it and never check on me again? I could be dead as far as he knows.

Men always want the best for me.

I wonder if any man ever wants the very best for any woman.

Men always want the best for me.

My stepfather probably wanted the best for me, but then he died, so he ended up leaving me too.

Day 2

Men always want the best for me.

This is pointless. No man wants the best for me. I don't even know if I want what's best for me.

Men always want the best for me.

My half brother Danny wants the best for me. At least he's one guy who does.

Day 3

Men always want the best for me.
I wish I hadn't promised Joan I'd do this every day.

Men always want the best for me.
What a waste of time.

Men always want the best for me.
I'm getting nothing today.

Men always want the best for me.
I'm quitting. This is stupid.

Day 4

Men always want the best for me.
Grandpa Allen always did want the best for me. There, I have two now, Grandpa and Danny.

Men always want the best for me.
If men want the very best for me, then why did Jack leave?

Day 5

Men always want the best for me.
Maybe there are some men who do want what's best for me.

Men always want the best for me.

Maybe it was best for me that Jack left. Maybe subconsciously he knew that.

Day 6

Men always want the best for me.

Maybe this is true. I just couldn't see through my own hurt enough to meet men who really do want the best for me.

Men always want the best for me.

I, Audrey, now only attract loving, supportive men who do want what's best for me.

Men always want the best for me.

I, Audrey, want the best for me. Therefore I only attract and accept into my life men who want the same.

Men always want the best for me.

Aunt Jane said that Daddy thought it was best to give me up for adoption by my stepfather. He thought it would be too confusing for me to have two daddies. I love you, Daddy. I have missed you so. I forgive you.

Men always want the best for me.

Yes, they do, and I do too!

At this point, Audrey had reached what I call the neutral point. You arrive at this juncture when you can begin to say "yes"

or at least "maybe." This is when the energy from the old negative and false beliefs begins to be released and the healing begins. You see, the spiritual truth is that in their God-selves, men
really do want the best for everyone. Only when Audrey was
healed of the subconscious need to be hurt or dumped on could
she draw men into her life who truly did want the best for her.

At this turnaround point, I suggest you write the affirmation fifteen to twenty times a day for a week. If any old residue
surfaces, be sure to clean it out by writing more responses.

Audrey made remarkable progress. And as happens when
we begin to clean out that lower nine-tenths, some remarkable
and miraculous things occurred.

Her father, whom she had not heard from in thirty years,
located her and sent a letter, stating that he hoped she was well
and happy and that he had been thinking about her a lot. He had
been living in Bali for some time. She still hasn't seen him, but
she corresponds with him and, more important, she no longer
lives from the energy of the abandoned little girl. When we dig
deep inside, examine our soul patterns, and allow ourselves to be
healed at our depths, it is astonishing what can happen.

When Audrey began her healing work on this issue, it
never occurred to her that her long-lost father would surface.
When we do the necessary healing work, we cannot imagine
what God has in store for us. No one could ever convince me
that Audrey's work and her father's unexpected contact were
unrelated.

Now that she is no longer coming out of the energy of the
abandoned four-year-old, she has been able to do further healing work. For the first time in her life, she is in a healthy, mature
relationship with a loving, supportive man. He truly does want
the very best for her.

Look within your own life for those negative core beliefs that you are already consciously aware of, those that would go into the upper one-tenth of the iceberg. If you are having difficulty identifying these core beliefs, seek the aid of a close friend who knows you well. Be certain you choose someone you view as emotionally healthy, rather than someone you suspect shares the same negative core beliefs as you.

I suggest you create your own iceberg diagram and make several copies. Put one in your purse or briefcase or car or tape it to your bathroom mirror at home, someplace where you, and only you, will see it often. Keep another copy with you wherever you go throughout the day, so that you can add to your list whenever a newly surfacing negative belief reaches your conscious awareness.

Making Your List

When you are ready to make your list, take some time to be alone and begin brainstorming. Don't discount anything that comes up. Take as much time as you need for soul-searching. Ask yourself what basic beliefs you have carried with you throughout your life that have no spiritual roots. Some examples would be:

I'm nothing without a man.

All women are phonies.

Trust no one.

Life's a bitch.

All men are crazy.

The only thing men are interested in is sex.

The only thing women are interested in is a man's credit card.

All women hate men.

All men hate women.

Once you have uncovered at least five or six negative core beliefs that belong in the tip of the iceberg, write them in the appropriate space. Use the diagram below to fill in the iceberg as it applies to your life.

At the tip, designated by the letter *A*, you can begin to process what is already known to you by, first, becoming aware of it each time it is present in your life and, second, beginning to turn the negative thought into a positive affirmation. It is important to realize that you do have the power to change and transform these old thoughts, beliefs, and patterns. You can begin to change the hurtful thoughts in *A* by flipping them from their upside-down, out-of-alignment-with-the-truth-of-your-being position to right side up, or right-mindedness. It is from here that you create the affirmation.

For example, if your negative belief is "Life is a bitch," then create an affirmation to counter that misperception, such as "Life is a wonder, and I am part of that wonder." A writing exercise using that affirmation could go something like this:

Life is a wonder, and I am part of that wonder.
Yeah, right!

Life is a wonder, and I am part of that wonder.
No way — no wonder in my life.

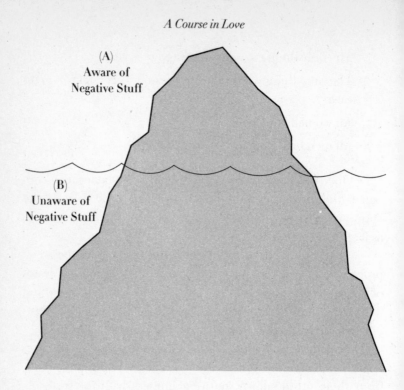

(A)
**Aware of
Negative Stuff**

(B)
**Unaware of
Negative Stuff**

Life is a wonder, and I am part of that wonder.
This is ridiculous.

Life is a wonder, and I am part of that wonder.
What a waste of time.

Life is a wonder, and I am part of that wonder.
My life's a bitch — no wonder there.

Life is a wonder, and I am part of that wonder.
I wish I could be.

Life is a wonder, and I am part of that wonder.
I wonder if this is true for anyone I know.

Life is a wonder, and I am part of that wonder.
I wish it could be true for me.

Life is a wonder, and I am part of that wonder.
Hmmm . . . maybe.

Life is a wonder, and I am part of that wonder.
I really would love to experience life as a wonder.

The actual writing would go through many more repetitions over days and weeks before you would reach that equalizing point where you begin to say, "Maybe, just maybe it could be so for me." This is the juncture at which your hardened defenses begin to crack. After that, you would continue to write until you were actually affirming the wonder of life for yourself.

Here are other examples: from "They are all out to get me," to "I now attract only loving and supportive people"; from "Trust no one," to "I trust my brothers and sisters who are one with me in God."

Work on part *A* issues whenever you become aware of them. Write each affirmation with its response until you come to a clear point where your response is in agreement with the affirmation. Be mindful not to program more garbage into the tip of the iceberg. This writing technique is like a spiritual Roto-rooter. It is a powerfully effective way to dislodge and release years of deeply buried negative beliefs that have repeatedly created upset, hurt, and failed relationships.

Now for part (*B*). As you work through the (*A*) segment of the iceberg, that which has been long buried will begin to rise to the surface. Pencil these recently revealed insights onto the (*B*) section of the diagram. The negative energy in part (*B*) is transformed through an unshakable commitment to do whatever is necessary to free yourself of this internalized guilt.

Although it may seem strange and at first outrageous, what we have actually done is value guilt. This, in turn, has led us to create a world in which attack is justified. The ego is always seeking to find and assign blame to the actions of others and self and sees sin rather than mistake and error. Guilt always damns and condemns.

The ego feeds from the guilt that lies in part (*B*). This is how it is kept alive to condemn one who has made a mistake, rather than seeing with compassionate eyes a sister or brother who temporarily is living out of fear. When we condemn and want to make another guilty, we too feel guilty and seek to condemn ourselves.

It is the hidden guilt in us that conceals the light of God from our awareness and keeps alive our attacks on one another and ourselves. These feelings of guilt induce fear of retaliation or abandonment and thus ensure that the future will continue to be like the past.

Release from this hidden guilt comes when we can see ourselves and one another as spiritual beings. Guilt stands in the way of our remembering who we truly are.

There is something I know to be true and often say, "God does not judge us; we have learned to do that job too well ourselves." In releasing these guilt feelings, we can begin to experience our own release from the chains of guilt and then experience the purity of God's loving embrace that has longed for our awakening.

This view of guilt goes far deeper in definition than the normal worldly concept of guilt. It teaches that the reason we see ourselves and everyone else as so guilty is that in separating ourselves into our own islands, we have felt such unbearable isolation that we could not tolerate our pain. So we hurled it outward, projecting what was in us upon everything and everyone who entered our narrow world. This action has made us feel very guilty, guilty on a soul level. This is not the guilt of eating a piece of chocolate cake and breaking your diet. It is guilt that has condemned you and all others to a hell on earth.

To free ourselves and others, we must turn the whole ugly mess over to our God-selves. Ask for the gentleness of God's healing love to softly flow through you. Take time to sit very still in meditation and visualize the light of love gently shining through the dark, heavy fog of guilt. Allow the light within you to expand and continue to erase the darkness of guilt. Breathe deeply, releasing the guilt that does not serve you. Affirm: "I release the guilt. There is only love." As love flows, it flushes out the dark fog. As this work continues through your forgiveness of this mistake, you are returned to your right mind and can experience the love that has been waiting for you.

Forgiving on such a deep inner level is a process that must be practiced in time and is already complete in eternity.

❧ 7 ❧

Recognizing Your "Stuff" and Working on It

Not long ago a young woman asked me, "What do you mean when you talk about working on yourself, working on your 'stuff'? What is there to work on?"

I use the word *stuff*, rather than the more common designation, to sum up the totality of our unhealed garbage. Whatever word you use, it is important to recognize that it's yours, not the other person's, and that there is work to be done on yourself. "Stuff" that needs to be healed can range from brooding rage toward your mother, to compulsive behavior, to being a controller or a manipulator, to behaving as a hurt child, to believing you're the victim of men, government, culture, or you-name-it. "Stuff" can be glaringly obvious or subtle and hidden under a veneer of "Everything is wonderful!"

Only what we withhold is lacking in any situation. This means that whenever we perceive that love, understanding, forgiveness, or sensitivity is lacking from a relationship, we personally are the ones who have not given a full measure of love, understanding, forgiveness, or sensitivity.

This teaching stands with no exceptions. Of course, we wish to make all sorts of exceptions, screaming in outrage that in our case it just cannot be so. We can protest, we can deny this truth, but our outcry does not alter it.

I don't know about you, but my ego really did not like this message, especially in the light of all the healing work I had done. As a result of that work, I was much happier and more complete, but I was still alone, when what I really wanted was to be living in a holy relationship with my soulmate. So I surrendered a bit more to the power of Divine Love and asked to be shown the way to give and receive love into my life more fully.

During this time I was beginning my second year of Mystery School with the noted humanistic psychologist Dr. Jean Houston. Every year Dr. Houston presents intensive training to a group of about 150 people, mostly professionals from around the world. Her work is patterned after that of the ancient mystery schools, which were training centers for initiation into the ancient religious and spiritual sciences. Weekends at the Mystery School were rich with myth and ritual, sacred dance and reenactment, and astonishing lectures by Dr. Houston, of whom Joseph Campbell said, "Her mind is our national treasure." I had attended and completed one whole year and still wanted to glean more, so I returned in January 1986 to begin year two.

On the second night of the first session, we participated in a spiritual initiation that went on well into the night. The gym where this work was conducted usually looks just like countless other gymnasiums—utilitarian, plain, angular, and cold—but in preparation for that night's activity, it underwent a metamorphosis. Luxurious fabrics, soft candlelight, and various artifacts and treasures from around the world all graced the space. The resulting creation pulsated warmth and a sense of the exotic, as the gym became a sacred temple out of ancient Athens or Thebes. Everything took on a shimmering, iridescent, otherworldly quality.

Starting around midnight, one at a time, each participant went before Jean and asked for what he or she desired from the year, from life, from the Mystery School experience. While this ritual was going on, the remaining participants slowly walked in a huge circle. After a student spoke with Jean, he or she was free to leave, so gradually, through the course of the evening, the size of the group dwindled. Each one moved into the center position as he or she felt moved to do so from within, governed by no external directive.

That night I slowly walked in that circle hour after hour. I knew what I had to ask for but still felt a little hesitancy, maybe a slight embarrassment. At 3:30 A.M., being one of the few students remaining, I inched my way into position within the inner circle before this Athenian woman of wisdom and power.

As we stood facing each other in what seemed like an instant of timelessness, she asked, "What do you want out of this year?" "Love, I want love. I want to meet the Beloved of My Soul with Skin On. I want to be with my soulmate." Her eyes pierced me—it was as if she was looking not at me, but at my soul. She began to speak, "You, a minister of love, ask now for love?" Yes, I nodded. Then she said something I certainly would never have expected, "I'm going to hit you." I was stunned. Jean is a large woman, nearly six feet tall, and strong. Using the heel of her right hand, she struck with full force my heart chakra. Thump! She stared through me again and said, "I'm going to hit you again." Thump! The tears came rolling down my cheeks as she said, "There! Now your heart is fully open to receive and give the love you desire."

It was truly one of the most bizarre experiences of my spiritual quest. I stepped away from Jean and continued to walk the circle, crying all the while. I wasn't crying because of pain from her blows, although they were quite forceful. I was crying tears of release.

Her striking my heart chakra had released some long-held fortification. It was as if a dam had burst. I walked until my personal waterfalls stopped, then returned to my room as dawn approached, absolutely knowing that something very significant had happened.

The blockade against love that had been there crumbled in that early morning hour. I was now fully ready to receive the love I desired and was capable of giving forth even more love.

Now I do not recommend that you and a couple of friends get together and pound on one another's heart centers. It was what was right for me, at that time. As you heal and open more and more, you too will be better in tune with what is right for you . . . and when.

Spirit is always guiding us toward our good. The more we practice trusting in a power greater than ourselves, the more we will experience our highest good. This highest good is always held out to us as a possibility, but until we are willing to get our self and our stuff out of the way, our good will remain just a possibility.

We are each individually and uniquely guided into that good. This does not preclude the need to do our inner work and discover those pieces that no longer fit. There will be many pieces for you to examine before your picture is complete. What is of primary importance is your willingness to complete each segment of the work.

Beginning Your Inner Work

To gain further insight into what particular work you are to do, examine your life carefully and thoroughly, looking with a Sherlock eye at the results right now in your life. Here is a technique that can be very helpful.

Look closely at what you perceive as negative and not working. These results are the effects. Write them down, each one separately, then go backward from there to get to the cause. What was the cause that produced the effect you are now experiencing? Remember, the cause lies in you: it may be hidden, but it is in there, somewhere in your thoughts and in your belief system. If you can honestly look for the cause, you will uncover the inner prompters that have withheld love and its full expression from your experience.

Chris, a nursing-home administrator, was finding herself short-tempered with her sons, irritated with her co-workers, and feeling put upon by bosses who disregarded her needs. In addition, she was bickering with her mother and sister, both of whom were upset with Chris over her latest romantic interest. It was yet another failed relationship, they reminded her.

Chris, who had just had a shouting match with her sister, was feeling that no one she knew respected her or considered her needs. Couldn't they see this was a difficult time for her? Why was she constantly surrounded by selfish people who always thought they had the right answer?

Distraught, Chris came to me seeking a spiritual solution. As we talked, I began to share with Chris the idea that what she was currently experiencing in her life was there to show her what needed to be healed within her. Chris said she was willing to explore whatever might be buried deeper, although she was quite sure the source of the problem was "out there" rather than in her.

Sitting quietly, she began to explore in broad, sweeping strokes what she had been experiencing repeatedly over the past several months.

1. She seemed to be forever noticing how self-consumed her friends and colleagues were.

2. On several occasions, she had felt that her motives were deeply misunderstood by others.

3. Three times recently, women had become very angry at her.

4. Her ongoing pattern of attracting and dating emotionally unavailable men had surfaced yet again.

Chris was no longer willing to live in her discomfort, nor was she willing to continue repeating these patterns. She was ready to uncover the underlying causes. After writing out the above list and more, Chris just sat with it for several days. Then, she began to explore the possible causes of the results she had listed.

1. She had been focusing an exorbitant amount of energy on herself, her wants, her preferences, what others were or were not doing for her or to her. Being brutally frank, she acknowledged that she had been just as self-consumed, if not more so, than those she had been judging.

2. As for others misunderstanding her motives, here she had a real "Aha!" Of course she had felt her motives were misunderstood. She was unclear within herself, and instead

of working on that issue, she had been busy taking an inventory of everyone else's faults.

3. Chris took the presence of angry women in her life as a clue that she must have a layer of her own unrecognized anger trying to surface. She didn't like it, but she was willing to look at it, heal it, and let it go.

4. She caught the reemergence of her old dating pattern very quickly, stopped the relationship, and did several forgiveness techniques on herself and the key players from her past. Then she surrounded all the men and herself in healing love.

Using this exercise will help you examine the current undesirable effects in your own life and show you how to take a closer look at what the causes are. Begin to look at the recurring themes in your life. Ask yourself with total honesty: what are the repetitive patterns in my life? List them. Then ask: what do I feel is being done to me? List what occurs to you. You can learn from these lists and reach a better understanding of what your stuff is made up of.

To move in consciousness to the level of being in tune with a soulmate, it is really helpful to unload yourself of excess baggage, to become free of your unhealed stuff. As I've said before, this is not easy, but it is worth all the work. Life takes on a sweetness as we touch the indescribable pure love that is our essence. Your world is filled with miracles. The stars will move for you. As we clear out the shadowy parts of ourselves, we begin to see the wonder of life that has been here just waiting for us. This kind of living isn't done with sleight of hand or mirror tricks. It is real.

When we are emotionally clear, when we have worked through our issues and healed the holes in our souls, when we at long last love ourselves, then we are radiant magnets of loving energy. We can attract love and let our own beauty out. When we love ourselves, we feel good enough about ourselves to allow our radiance and attractiveness to be seen by other people. We no longer need or desire to keep this aliveness cloaked in the darkness of old hurts, sorrows, and grievances.

Most of us have done what Jesus spoke of. We have taken a bushel basket and put it over our light. When you feel really good about your true self, you'll take the bushel basket off and *wow!* There you are in all your radiant splendor!

We must love ourselves in order to allow ourselves to be attractive and radiate an energy of warmth, love, and receptivity. We don't love ourselves in an ego-based way, but rather in a divinely centered way, a way in which we no longer condemn ourselves to live half a life.

I have seen people, women and men, transformed from weeds into lilies as their negative patterns begin to heal. Sadness leaves the eyes and face. The brow relaxes permanently. A slumping posture straightens. Instead of drooping, shoulders are broad and square. Health improves; little cuts, bruises, and scrapes from constantly beating on oneself go away. Observe how, when you are self-critical, you are forever running into chairs, cupboards, and doors. You are constantly tripping or falling down. One friend of mine finally made the connection between minor kitchen burns and her always saying that her boyfriend's behavior "just burned her up." The light dawned, and she ceased having a relationship with that man. Immediately she was kinder to herself and no longer had the need to inflict burns on herself.

Many amazing results, both subtle and profound, occur as we learn to love ourselves. My dear friend Linda, who had suffered sexual abuse from her stepfather throughout her childhood, realized after years of healing her trauma and pain that her eyes changed from sad, murky brown to green and radiant with light. "I now feel the bliss of God in the cells and energy of my body," she says. Many report bliss in their bodies. One woman I know said she was so alive she felt like she was "carbonated." We cannot have an experience of profound inner healing without there being some very noticeable inner and outer effects. When we love ourselves and feel good about ourselves, we allow our beauty to be seen by others.

I have never met a truly unattractive person, but I've met countless people who felt lousy about themselves and would not allow themselves to be attractive. Every one of us is a *natural* beauty. Beauty has not been measured out to a select few; it's available to anyone who believes that he or she is deserving enough to be attractive and radiate an inner beauty. We all possess an innate beauty. I'm not speaking of some artificial, phony kind of mask, but the beauty that comes from the inside out.

There are no unattractive people, just folks with some very unattractive thoughts about themselves. A most beautiful thought was expressed by Baldassare Castiglione, "Beauty, I believe, comes from God. Therefore, there can be no beauty without goodness."

When we have touched the spirit within us, we just automatically begin to see ourselves as attractive and become irresistibly attractive to others. Others recognize that we have a certain "something." They may not understand or know just what it is, but they will know they want to be around it.

When I released the woman who had been locked in the attic of my mind, my entire physical appearance and presentation changed. I allowed a softness to come out that had always been there, but of which I had been afraid. I had been afraid that it would make me look weak, but what it really did was make me more attractive and spiritually powerful.

There is much that you can do to prepare for your holy relationship, and learning to truly love and respect yourself is a giant stride in the right direction. To learn to love ourselves, we must first come into a holy relationship with our self, our divine self. We must learn to recognize our stuff when it's present in our lives. We must be willing to do the work necessary to be healed and to release the wonderful self that is inside us.

I'm in Pain—Whose Fault Is It?

We seek to find the root cause of our problem, our pain, not so that we can assign blame, but so that we can gain insight. We do it so that we can understand the hidden dynamics that have been at work creating our current view of reality. It is here that we begin to forgive—forgive the other person or people, forgive the situation for our perceived pain, forgive ourselves for allowing the situation to be. Then we go on. As we do all this, we are releasing the energy patterns that have repeatedly created the same scenario in our lives.

Have you noticed the same painful type of situation occurring over and over in your life? The people may be different, the circumstances slightly altered, and the setting new, but the dynamic of what is happening remains exactly the same. Once again you find yourself abandoned, abused, or dumped, and the pain doesn't diminish just because the pattern has become familiar.

We use our grievances to close our eyes and stop up our ears. We see what we want to see and hear what we want to hear. What we see and hear may or may not have anything to do with reality. When we are holding grievances, we take everything we see or hear as a personal attack on our little kingdom or queendom. We believe its sole function is to attack our peace of mind. When our minds cling to grievances, we take everything personally, whether it be a sideways glance or an offhand comment. Any minuscule slight becomes more ammunition in our arsenal of grievances.

The spiritually mature have learned to take nothing personally. They are part of what I like to think of as the Ah So School of Mastery. There are many "ah so" stories originating in ancient Eastern wisdom. Here is one of my favorites:

A young woman and her angry parents show up at the door of a monastery demanding to see a certain young monk. When the monk presents himself, the parents pull forward their obviously pregnant daughter and say she has confessed that he is the father of her child. The monk simply responds, "Ah so." The father, now further outraged, says that when the baby is born he will take it from his daughter and give it to the monk, who will be responsible for raising the child within the monastery. The monk responds, "Ah so." The family leaves and the monk without a word returns to his duties. Several months later, the father returns and thrusts a newborn baby into the monk's arms. The young monk looks into the face of the child and says, "Ah so." The monk tenderly cares for the newborn in his tiny cell. Time passes and the parents, the daughter, and a young man arrive at the door of the monastery. This time the father says his daughter was in anguish without her child, came to him, and confessed it was not the monk who was the father of the child, but this young man who had been her lover. She had been afraid of her father's wrath against the boy and had made up the story about the monk. They say they are in love and cannot bear to live without their baby. Will the young monk please forgive them and return the child, to which he responds, "Ah so," as he gives back the infant.

To stay centered no matter what is going on around you, not to take personally what another says or does, is true emotional freedom. The next time you are about to take personally someone's comment or slight, simply utter, "Ah so," and go about your life.

8

Forgive, Forgive, Forgive

You can have happiness, a quiet mind, clear purpose, beauty beyond this world, sure protection, undisturbed tranquillity, constant gentleness, and anything else wonderful and positive you can imagine. Sound unbelievable? Not according to *A Course in Miracles,* which states: "All this forgiveness offers you, and more." In fact, the *Course* says, "Forgiveness offers everything I want."

Well, I jumped on that one! Yes, I wanted happiness, a quiet mind, a certainty of purpose, along with beauty, peace, gentleness, comfort, and rest, and I wanted more. I wanted a loving, supportive relationship. I wanted to meet my soulmate. I wanted to be happily, joyfully married. I wanted to be in a relationship that was a joy, easy, not competitive or a struggle. I wanted to be in a relationship that was holy.

True forgiveness involves really getting into your psyche and processing what has long been your unresolved conflict, that bottom nine-tenths of the iceberg. It means discovering the prompters, such as certain behaviors, attitudes, personalities, or situations, that propel you into knee-jerk reactions. It also entails examining family patterns and generational dysfunctional behaviors.

Is all this necessary to have a relationship with your soulmate? Yes, if you want it to be a healthy, happy, easy, and lasting one.

After I left my second husband, I knew that if I was ever to have true love and be healed, I had to get to the core of my psyche to discover why I had chosen two partners who were so challenging. It was a compelling mission, and at times it seemed impossible. But all things are possible when certainty of purpose and clarity of intention are coupled with Divine Love. And I was determined to get to the core, heal it, and be free.

So what was going on deep inside that caused me to repeat the same mistake? A normal course of action is to examine one's early relationships with parents and uncover where negative beliefs and patterns could have originated. Had I married my mother or father? Well, I did this nearly endlessly and got some minor insights, but never a full "Aha!" I never experienced an earth-shattering, mind-blowing realization that shouted through my being, "This is it!" No "aha" here.

Then one weekend a workshop facilitator was working with me on this issue and asked a question I had never explored before. Had any male relative or family friend lived with my family when I was a child? Slowly the light began to dawn and then the full impact hit me. I had married Uncle Tony—not literally, of course, but a man very much like he had been.

When I was a child my mother's younger brother would spend nearly every weekend with our family. He was a handsome, charming, flashy young man who drove a silver Jaguar and had a cutting wit. He would take me for rides in his traffic stopper of a car, driving at one hundred miles per hour while I squealed in mixed terror and fascination. Then he would buy me an ice cream cone or some little trinket and everything was supposed to be just fine again.

Uncle Tony always favored me and would pour on the charm. I never could totally relax with him, though, because he was quick to anger, and when he was angry he was not much fun anymore. As I got to be a little older, I realized that every month or so he was with a different woman. My mom said he was a ladies' man. I didn't know what that meant. Once I noticed black-and-blue marks on one of his girlfriend's upper arms. When I asked her what happened, she said she had fallen and Tony had caught her. It seemed a funny place to have bruises. Then there was another woman with more bruises, and I just knew something wasn't right. But at nine years old I was too young to figure it out.

Whenever I'd question my uncle, he'd just make a joke and I'd giggle and think he was so funny, never understanding this adult dynamic. When I was about sixteen, my mother and uncle had an argument and he left our lives forever. We heard he moved to California, then out of the country, and we never heard a word from him again. I had been his favorite niece, had seen him all the time, and then never again.

A few years ago I tracked down his phone number and called him in California, where he was living. He was speechless at learning who was on the other end of the line. He said he was coming to the town where I was staying that weekend and would call me at the hotel and set a time to meet. I checked the front desk for messages several times. There were none, and it was then I realized he would never call. He never did.

My uncle was all flash and show on the outside without much depth or genuine caring on the inside. He had a charming veneer, was handsome and dapper on the outside, but he also was critical, manipulative, highly dysfunctional in his relationships with women, egocentric, and sitting on a raging inferno of hostility toward all women. He was emotionally and physically abusive. In my child mind I filed away all these characteristics, and years later I found a mate who, while not identical to Uncle Tony, was a pretty good reflection of him.

I had already done a great deal of work forgiving him and his erratic treatment of me as a child. The flashiness, the all-show-and-no-substance that I had re-created in my adult life, made sense now. Once I understood that I had "married my uncle," married what repelled and attracted me as a child, I was able to direct my healing work where it was most needed. It wasn't just my former husband I needed to forgive; there was also more work to do with my uncle and myself.

My former husband was the tip of the iceberg, the one-tenth. My uncle and I were the previously hidden nine-tenths that had been buried deep in my soul-memory and psyche. Those deep hurts out of the past are what create the wounds of the soul.

It often takes some real digging to discover what the root cause has been. Sometimes it is revealed to us. Sometimes we'll never know the specific cause, but we become aware of the effects and through forgiveness can uproot the cause without ever consciously knowing what it was.

Forgiveness is the lesson we are here to learn. We all have teachers of forgiveness. Some play minor roles while others occupy the major ones. I'm sure you've had yours, just as I've had mine, some of whom I've shared with you in this book. They keep teaching us day after day, through all our time with them, until we realize that what we need to do is forgive these people, not hate or withdraw, not ignore them or throw them out of our hearts.

My husband, David, tells how he worked for decades to forgive his mother. His mother, Edith, was a yeller. She'd yell at the neighbors, the repairman, and the meter reader. As a small boy, David would retreat in embarrassment whenever this happened. When she yelled at his father, he would hide. She never hit or punished David, but oh, how she'd yell.

As David grew up and his mother kept yelling and continued to be his teacher, he realized that he did not hold a lot of love for her in his heart. This withholding was blocking his flow of love to others. It was affecting his adult life and it was hurting him. He didn't know what to do until he realized that his only choice was to forgive her. That was at a time when he knew he had to do something to resolve his feelings toward his mother, so he began to hold the affirmation, "I forgive you, Mother, for yelling." All of a sudden, when he saw her, he realized her yelling was quieter to his ears. He worked daily to completely forgive her, and in the ensuing years no matter what she did or how much she yelled, it had no effect on him.

Meanwhile, Edith kept yelling. David's resolved feelings were within him, and in his case they did not spill over to his mother. Owing to a stroke, she spent her last fifteen years in a very caring, loving nursing facility. She yelled at everyone there, the nurses, the aides, the doctors; she even yelled at the minister who was responsible for her being in this lovely home.

Edith must have had a great deal of love in her, too, because she attracted many kind, loving people into her life. Then at ninety-one years of age, her teaching and learning time on earth completed, she gently slipped from this physical plane. At her wake, her primary caregiver, who just adored this crotchety old woman, came up to the casket all teary-eyed, looked in for a long time, then turned to David and said, "Well, it looks like Edith, but she's not yelling!"

It took death to silence Edith. David's joy was that before her death he had lost, through forgiveness, his reason to be upset with her. Again and again, he would hold a loving thought of forgiveness directed toward his mother.

If you have wondered what you are doing on this planet, now your question has been answered. You, dear one, are here to forgive. Whatever has happened in your life has occurred to support you in learning this one lesson. Each player upon the stage of your life's drama that has upset you in any way came into the play at your subconscious request, to give you the opportunity to learn the lesson of forgiveness.

Now you have to admit some of the players have given Academy Award–winning performances. Your function is not to judge them, criticize them, ignore them, or present them with an Oscar. Your function is to forgive them. You can never have a holy relationship in your life when you hold unforgiveness within your heart.

The idea that we must forgive everyone and everything can be a very upsetting thought for some. They see the particular details of their situation as so horrific that forgiveness would somehow say it didn't matter, or would discount their feelings or experiences. What forgiveness does is allow us to see our past in a totally new light with a totally new awareness. Forgiveness frees us from the past and from reliving again and again the horror, outrage, pain, and sorrow. Until we come to the place of total forgiveness, the unresolved situation continues to live within us and to negatively affect every relationship we have.

If you want a holy relationship, to live in joy with your soulmate, you have to forgive. It seems nearly impossible to realize that you must do it not for the other person's sake, but for your own. Your unforgiveness is polluting your life. Unforgiveness fills our lives and world with rotten, decaying energy. It clouds all we see and blinds us to our ever-present blessings and the beauty of life. It is important to realize that we all need to forgive ourselves. Because our judgments and grievances of self can run deep, self-forgiveness is often more difficult than forgiving others. All forgiveness techniques can be inner directed until a state of peace and a sense of clearing has been realized. Regardless of how difficult it may be for you to forgive yourself, this process is absolutely necessary for your total healing.

Focus on the Big One Until You Get It

You won't have to do much searching to get who the leading lady or starring man is in your personal drama of forgiveness. I am sure you already have some clear insight into who (or perhaps what) has given the star performance in your life. For David, it was his mother. For me, it was my second husband, who was a reflection of my uncle. For all of us, it is ourselves.

I worked for years to forgive my second husband. I wrote a forgiveness list many mornings for nearly five years. Yes, I was intent on removing this boulder to love. For me, there was no other way to get to the mother lode of ugliness buried in the bottom nine-tenths of the iceberg.

This kind of forgiveness work is very effective and one of my favorites. Each morning before doing anything else, sit quietly with a legal pad and pencil. Close your eyes and focus on one particular person with whom you have had a great deal of conflict and many grievances. When you are clear who the person is, open your eyes and take pad and pencil in hand.

I begin writing this way: "I, Joan, forgive myself. I forgive everyone. I am free, I am free." Then choose the subject (actor) of the day and continue writing. You need to be as specific as your memory is regarding the particular issues. For example, if your father was an alcoholic, rather than writing, "I now forgive you, Dad," write: "I forgive you, Dad, for coming home drunk nearly every night. I forgive you for missing my birthday. I forgive you for embarrassing me in front of my friends. I forgive you for being mean to Mom and making her cry. I forgive you for your life being such a mess. I forgive you for being so unhappy." Get really specific: "I forgive you for being a falling-down drunk at my college graduation. I forgive you for breaking every promise you ever made. I forgive you for polluting yourself every day with alcohol."

After you spend twenty, or preferably thirty, minutes writing this list, take it to the fireplace or the kitchen sink and burn it. The burning symbolizes a total change in form of the things on which you are working: from the writings on paper (something) into ashes (nothing). Then go back and sit down, meditate, and ask the peace of God to fill your being and Divine Love to flood you with the light of love. Breathe deeply and allow the healing activity of peace and love to take place within you. Do this part for at least ten minutes. Then get up and go much clearer into your day.

How long do you do this? Do it until you feel love and sense that the negativity within you is gone. Don't do it more than three times a week, or you'll bring up too much that needs to be processed at one time. Forgiveness involves changing your perception about the other person or situation. You'll know when this has happened, when no matter what that person does, it no longer upsets you. It might take you a month; it might take five years of writing and burning forgiveness lists. However long it takes, you will be thankful once forgiveness comes into your life and you are free.

I am reminded of the tourist who stops a New Yorker and asks how to get to Carnegie Hall. The New Yorker responds, "Practice, practice, practice." The forgiveness process obviously takes some diligence, but just like a piano concert at Carnegie Hall, the result will have been worth all the work. Amazing results will follow.

The most amazing result I have had from healing the past through forgiveness work began while David and I were in Hawaii setting up a spiritual tour to those mystical islands. There, the thought of my former husband kept coming to mind. This was very perplexing to me and I told David about it, saying, "I really don't think this is about needing to forgive him. I'm confused as to why he keeps coming into my mind." David considered this a moment and then said, "Maybe he's coming to you for a blessing. Just send him some blessings."

This sounded good to me, so I did that and thought nothing else about it until returning home. The first Monday home I had an early-morning appointment with my hair stylist, who greeted me at the door nearly breathless and said, "I'm so glad you're here! Your ex-husband [he still went to my stylist] was in last week and said he really wanted to contact you but was afraid that you might not speak to him if he called. He's in the hospital having quadruple bypass surgery, beginning right this very moment, and he's very scared. He wanted me to ask you to please pray for him if you could find it in your heart to do that."

I said of course I would, and began to hold him in God's light and healing presence—thinking to myself, he had contacted me, he just hadn't used the telephone.

Two days later I was making hospital visits to several members of my congregation who were in neighboring facilities when I got a crystal-clear message, "Go visit him in the hospital." Laughing, I said out loud to whomever was sending me this message inside my head, "You must have me confused with some very holy person." The message was repeated, "Go see him now!" This time it was very emphatic.

Well, by this point in my life I had learned to listen to and follow my inner directives. So off to that hospital I drove, getting lost on the way—even though it was only three blocks away. I listened and followed. I did not say I was free from resistance.

He was in the Cardiac Intensive Care Unit and a nurse led me right to his cubicle, thinking I was his minister. I asked the Holy Spirit to be with me as I slowly opened the drawn curtain and stood at the end of his bed. The poor man almost had further heart problems at the shock of seeing me after so many years and so much hurt. He kept saying, "I can't believe you came to see me. I can't believe you came to see me."

As I looked at him, I saw he was one very sick man. I walked over and took his hand, just as I had done with the other patients I had visited that morning. "Oh, Joan," he said, "can you ever forgive me?" Before I could answer, he went on, "I was such a shit to you. Can you ever forgive me?" At that point I stopped him and asked him to please not talk, he didn't need to say those things. He answered, "Yes, I do, I do need to ask for your forgiveness after all that I did. I was such a shit to you."

I responded, "I have already forgiven you. I could not have come here had I not."

He looked as if a heavy burden had been lifted, and I asked if he would like us to pray together. "Yes, very much so," he responded. He was on this most unusual low bed, and in order to hold both his hands and pray, I had to kneel down. (Does God have an outrageous sense of humor or what!) As we prayed for the healing of his physical heart, I knew both of our inner hearts were being healed in those moments.

While praying, I became aware of a light brightly shining within that cubicle. Opening my eyes, I saw that we both, he lying in recovery and I kneeling at the side of this man I had once feared and loathed, were enfolded in a bright golden light. There was no window and no overhead light. The light wasn't within the whole space, but was like a cotton-candy gauze around the two of us.

In those moments I knew I had totally forgiven my former husband and he me. We had experienced a miracle.

When we have forgiven fully, the cause of the upset is no longer an impediment in our lives. The situation may or may not change in the outer, but it has changed and changed permanently in the inner.

This does not occur for us in one wiping of the cloth. Now you may be the exception, but please remember the iceberg. Forgiveness is a process, not a solitary act. Our grievances are stratified through many layers of our psyches, our conscious and subconscious minds. We must, through forgiveness, cleanse thoroughly until we clear each of the layers. This is work, especially in the early years of practicing forgiveness. It is practice, like learning to play a musical instrument or mastering the chessboard. Remember, just as mastery of the piano and a concert at Carnegie Hall do not come in an afternoon, neither does complete forgiveness.

A dear woman, Brenda, made an appointment to see me, saying she needed some instructions for a project she was working on that weekend. She certainly piqued my curiosity and as she settled in, I asked what the "project" was and how she saw me helping. Brenda began by saying she had three full days alone without her three children, who would be spending time with their dad, her former husband. She was going to put the days to good use: her calendar was clear, and she was going to forgive her former husband over the weekend! I was quiet for a bit and then said, "Perhaps I missed something here. Tell me again what you are going to do over the next three days?"

"Well," she said, "I've really gotten how important it is that I forgive my ex and release him to his new life and wife. My anger and rage at him have only really hurt me and not him and I get that now. So I'm going to take the next three days, with no kids, unplug the phone and TV, and I'm going to forgive him."

"Brenda, how long were you married?" I inquired.

"Seventeen years, but it really was over after four or five. I just kept hoping the situation would change or he would change. I guess I stayed for the kids and because I was afraid to go out on my own. But now that he's gone, life is so much more peaceful and I'm making great money—more than him, so he quit paying child support. He says he can't afford to pay us, and I've threatened to pull him into court so he'll pay."

"Brenda," I interjected, "you were married to this man for seventeen years, you have three teenagers, he is now remarried and supporting his new family and can't afford child support. This may be a shock to you, but it will take more than a weekend of forgiveness to clear up this energy. This situation was seventeen years in the making, and I've never known or heard of the slate being wiped clean in a couple of days."

Forgiveness is not a quick fix, but it is a permanent, life-transforming process. Forgiving *is* forgetting. I truly can no longer remember the details of the grievances from the past. When we have completed our forgiveness work, our memory of the situation fades. If you can still recount all the sordid details like a litany, you have not forgiven. Do not deceive yourself with the ego's belief that it is possible to forgive and not forget. That is not true forgiveness. That is just a maneuver of the ego to keep the real cause of upset hidden from your awareness. Forgiveness is either complete or we still have work to do.

When we practice the lessons of forgiveness, we learn to see past the error from the inception and then the error never affects us again. We come to see that the one we viewed as perpetrator was really a wounded, unhealed, lost, and confused soul. Yes, maybe this confused soul did some cruel, thoughtless, and unloving deeds, but he or she did not understand the damage he or she was doing. It was as if the person were sleepwalking or even totally asleep.

Releasing Negative Energy

Until we awaken spiritually, we are asleep to our true worth and self, and we can behave quite insanely. Spiritually, then, we can say that such behavior is unreal, because of its own accord it has no reality and only appears to be real. In these instances, when we forgive, the heavy, dense energy that has been firmly held around the situations moves out, and light enters our consciousness.

Forgiveness is release from all illusions. Forgiveness transforms our vision and allows us to see clearly the world of peace, beauty, and love. If you want a life filled with an easy-flowing order, loving relationships, and abundance in every area, your course of action is to always forgive and to do it as quickly as possible.

I studied with a spiritual teacher, Dennis Adams, who later became my personal friend and who always taught that if you can catch a negative energy charge—a judgment, grievance, hurt, or upset—within three seconds and instantly release it to Divine Love, then the work is done. If you wait longer than three seconds, it will have already attached its sticky little tentacles to you, and it will take some work to get them off. Do your utmost to forgive as quickly as possible. It could save you years of work later.

A simple forgiveness technique is to affirm the person's name with the statement: "John, I forgive you, I bless you, I release you, I love you, I set you free." Memorize the affirmation, and anytime an old, unforgiving thought arises in your mind, repeat the affirmation several times to let the thought go.

Another effective forgiveness technique is to go to a quiet spot, have a meditative tape playing softly, and gently enter a state of quiet or meditation. See yourself surrounded by many gray clouds, each cloud representing an unforgiving thought, attitude, or feeling. Have the clouds form a thick ring around you.

When you can clearly picture this, bring yourself into the image and begin to gently brush the clouds aside as you move toward the center, to which you are being drawn by a radiant light. As you continue to brush the clouds aside, the light in the center becomes brighter and brighter. In this intensifying radiance, the remaining clouds begin to dissipate. You are now moving freely through the clouds of unforgiveness, able easily to sweep them aside. They have no substance. They are like mist dissolving in the sunlight. They are only clouds. Clouds cannot stop you.

Move through the clouds until you come fully into the light. Then remain very still and enter into a holy union with the light, allowing it to fill you and all the space previously occupied by your old unforgiving thoughts. Continue to fill yourself with the light. Breathe it in and out deeply, visualizing it filling you. Then simply rest and be still awhile. Be filled. Be healed. Be at peace. Be free.

Look honestly at the grievances and unforgiving thoughts that have kept you in the negative, repetitive patterns of your life. Ask yourself if you want the upset, the anger, the hatred, or if you want peace of mind, a quiet calm, and love to come into your life.

The situation may have begun when you were only four and had no control, but you do have control today. Today you decide whether to continue living as a wounded child or to live as an empowered adult who is free from the past. Consider what you want and remember: Forgiveness offers it. Forgiveness offers everything you want, and more.

9

Visualize, Pray, Meditate

When I was growing up, God and the spiritual and religious side of life were always important to me. In those formative years, though, I had very little understanding of the spiritual and a very formal training in the religious. Through my personal spiritual journey I have come to understand the distinction. The religious is taught, while the spiritual is experienced.

The religious teaches what others say about God, Buddha, Allah, Jesus, scripture. It is having a rote understanding of scripture without necessarily being able to apply its inner message to one's own life in a personal way.

The spiritual path is experienced by coming into alignment with the higher order of being. It is aligning spirit, soul, and body with the Higher Power. It is studying the spiritual laws that lie beneath the great religious and spiritual leaders' teachings. Then one learns, grows, and discovers more and more about one's own spiritual nature. This is the path I have come to walk. This is the path I teach.

The spiritual path is about becoming mature on a deep, inner level, taking full responsibility for whatever shows up in our lives. It is about keeping commitments and surrendering to the Higher Power. It is learning to listen to our inner guidance and having the faith to follow that guidance. It is also trusting that same Spirit to guide and direct our loved ones and all others. It is about living in integrity and our word being our honor.

To walk upon the spiritual path means to be quick to forgive and slow to judge, to look for the good and to be a blessing through your thoughts, words, and actions, through the very gaze of your eyes. It is to awaken from a long and deep sleep and claim your heritage as a beloved daughter or son of God.

The spiritual law of attraction states: Be what you want to attract. If you want love, be loving. If you want compassion, be compassionate. If you want kindness, be kind. If you want respect, be respectful.

Once a young woman wanting very much to be married went to see Charles Fillmore, the cofounder of the Unity movement, and asked him to pray with her that she would meet her perfect partner. After carefully considering her request, he said, "If you want to meet the perfect person, you must become the perfect person." Each of us must become what we want to attract.

The List

We must become what we want to attract. With this thought in mind, let's look at how to create a description of the attributes and characteristics of your perfect partner. Many experts in the helping professions argue that there is no such thing as a perfect person, let alone a perfect partner. Your perfect partner is the one who would be perfect for you. Isn't it curious how loudly we will argue for our littleness, insisting that what we desire is impossible to have? Yes, there is a perfect person for you. That doesn't mean that he'll never burp, that she'll never get upset, but it does mean that your souls' purposes are aligned.

To begin this exercise, get a pen and several sheets of clean paper. Now find a comfortable spot and allow yourself to relax, getting in touch with your inner knowing. When you feel really connected, start to write. Do this part as a brainstorming session with yourself. Write what is important to you, and remember that what you write on your list may not be at all important to someone else.

My list for David had forty-three points on it, and I'm happy to say he embodies them all. Here is what my list looked like:

Christ consciousness, kind, loving, tender, sincere, generous, faithful, compatible age, refined, intelligent, well educated, unencumbered, similar diet, non-meateater, great sense of humor, expressive, likes to travel, compatible sun sign, happy and up personality, thoughtful, gets who I am, straight, available, fun-loving, healthy, sensuous, sexy, supportive of me and my work, enjoys the arts, knows which fork to use, seeking me, ready for a commitment, first-class taste and wallet, similar interests, an active Truth student, functional, emotionally healthy, has worked through his stuff, cares about people, lets his beauty out, ready for a holy relationship, easy to be with.

I kept my list on an index card and, looking at it, I would affirm, "Thank you God for manifesting my perfect partner in my life now." I have taught this technique to thousands, and some have reported that their lists resulted in meeting their perfect partner in as little as three weeks. It took me longer than that, but remember we are working in universal time where the outcome will be perfect.

Work with the list as long as it feels right for you. Make changes and corrections, and when you feel that you've "got it," put the list away in a holy place. That may be in your Bible or other favorite book of spiritual teachings. I put mine in *A Course in Miracles.* Look at your list from time to time to be sure that what you wrote there is still important to you. It's okay to revise it from time to time.

The important thing to remember is that you are the counterpart of whatever you have chosen for your list. If you desire kindness, you need to be kind in all your encounters. If you seek tenderness, soften out any rough edges. If you want to be treated generously, check yourself out: if you are counting change, you have some work to do.

I'm sure you get the point. You need to become what you want to attract. Your being the counterpart will draw to you the desire of your heart. Recall Charles Fillmore's words and become the person you're looking for in a perfect partner. Be sure that after your list is complete, you embody or at least are working on becoming that which you hope to attract. Remember, like attracts like.

At a soulmate workshop that David and I teach around the country, where singles and couples join us for a day of discovery, healing, clarification, release, love, and joy, one of the participants was Joanne, a woman in her fifties. Joanne recounted how she had been happily married for over thirty years and had been widowed six months previously. She knew she had been married to a soulmate and knew what that kind of love was like. She also knew there must be another soulmate out there for her. She made her list and prayed and affirmed to attract a loving, dedicated, available new mate whom she would marry and live with in bliss.

Joanne is an amazing woman with a positive attitude. She just knew God did not want her to be alone for the rest of her life. She made her list and within two months she met her new husband. When I saw her recently, she reported they had just celebrated their first wedding anniversary and are very happy together. She honors the memory of her first love and delights in her new love.

Now, not everyone manifests his or her beloved as quickly as Joanne did, but when you can have the same openness and certainty as she had, it will happen.

God's desire for all of us is that we be happy. If you believe that living in a holy union would add to your happiness, all of life will support you in achieving your heart's desire. Holiness and happiness in our relationships are realized through forgiveness, belief, faith, and vision.

Visualization

Much has been written about the power of visualization. Practicing the art of visualization is really practicing seeing as God sees. God always sees the perfect pattern, beholds the perfect image. That is why after making your list, it is helpful to adjust it until you truly sense it is in alignment with the divine.

When you feel you have reached this point, find a quiet time and a place where you will not be disturbed. Sit down, relax, and take a few deep breaths in and out. Quiet your mind. Begin to fill your heart with the warm glow of love as you fill your mind with light—bright, clear, radiant light.

Now picture yourself being with your beloved in some happy, joyous situation. Do this until you can absorb the feeling of the other person and the two of you being together. Sense what the energy of the two of you being together would feel like. This may take a number of practice sessions before you can begin to sense your energy reaching out beyond your margins and connecting with your soulmate.

This visualization technique is painting an image in your conscious mind, as well as in your subconscious mind. Thoughts held in mind produce after their kind. Images held in mind produce after their kind.

When you hold the image in mind, through visualizing what you desire, you begin to breathe life into that image. Through practice, in time, that image moves from within your mind to within your experience. In other words, it moves from an inner picture to an outer manifestation.

When I practiced this before actually meeting David, I became so certain that he too was seeking me that I absolutely knew what being in his presence would feel like. When we met, I had an immediate recognition of his spiritual essence and a familiarity with his feeling, but it took me a few days to get comfortable with his physical form. I was not in tune with that part of him before our actual meeting.

One couple shared with me a similar experience. The woman had picked up at the airport an executive who was coming to town for an important meeting. As she was driving him to the meeting, they were stopped at a traffic light, sitting in silence, when all of a sudden she felt this loving, warm energy rolling off him. This "presence" was exactly the same as she had experienced during her morning prayer time and visualization practice.

She is a petite, charmingly humorous Frenchwoman with a heavy accent. As she tells the story, she slowly turned and looked at him as he was looking forward. She squinted and then took another little peek. "Nope, it sure doesn't look like 'him.'" Then she closed her eyes again. "But it sure feels like him."

In the next few days, they had a number of opportunities to speak briefly. Then, on his last evening in town, he asked her to dinner. As they say, the rest is history. Joseph's version of the story is that he knew instantly that Lydia was his soulmate. As he was staring out the window during their first encounter, he too was checking out her energy and knew she was the one he had been visualizing and praying for. He knew by the feel of her essence that she was the one.

Visualization works best when it is coupled with prayer. Prayer is our opportunity to talk to God. I am not one for formal prayers. In fact, I imagine that they bore God as much as they bore me. God doesn't need thee's and thou's and that stuffy language. God doesn't need anything. We need to know God and have a sense of his/her presence. Formal rhetoric and litanies will not do it for many of us. We should use the language that we are most comfortable with. We should always be comfortable when praying.

Prayer

Prayer is simply a way of asking for something. We need to get over any notion we may have that prayer changes God. Prayer changes us. God is not some big guy in the sky granting favors to a select few and ignoring the rest. All prayer is answered, but we do not always hear the response, or like what we hear.

We pray "amiss" when we plead with God, when we bargain and beseech. At one time or another, we have all attempted to strike a deal with God. You do this wonderful thing for me, God, you grant me this favor, and I will be a better person—no longer lie, swear, overeat, or whatever bargain we are willing to make.

God doesn't play some cosmic "Let's Make a Deal" with you. God loves you and has already given you everything—most importantly, free will that allows you to be and do whatever you want to be and do. What prayer can do is help you recognize that this is so.

In Unity and in other spiritual/metaphysical paths, we use affirmative prayer. We affirm aloud or write a positive statement of truth that assists us in aligning our personal natures with our spiritual nature. This affirmative prayer goes from an individual level to a universal level.

A Unity affirmation, "There is only one presence and one power in my life and in the universe, God, the good, omnipotent," is repeated by millions each week. It is a prayer to align our thinking and feelings with God's presence and power, to remind us once again that God is the only power.

A personal affirmation that reflects the theme of this book would be, "I am one with Divine Love. Divine Love now draws to me my own." I used this affirmation as I was healing and forgiving my past and getting ready for my soulmate. I highly recommend it!

Below is a list of some great affirmations. Remember, you may simply, mindfully state these aloud or silently. Or you may choose to write them, or even type them into a computer (just be sure you don't use the Copy command instead of typing the affirmation over and over). I suggest you make each one personal by inserting your own first name.

I, _____, am a spiritual being, living in a spiritual universe, governed by spiritual law.

I, _____, am love.

I, _____, am peace.

I, _____, am forgiving and free.

I, _____, am healing my past now.

The more I, _____, forgive and release my past, the more happy and free I become.

It is safe for me, _____, to live from a place of love.

It is safe for me, _____, to love.

Others joyously love and support the new me.

I, _____, now attract only kind, loving, and supportive men/women.

It is easy for me, _____, to love.

It is easy for me, _____, to forgive.

It is easy for me, _____, to heal.

It is easy for me, _____, to let go of the past.

We do not affirm to make something true. We affirm to remind ourselves of what is spiritually true. Remember, the affirmation brings your thoughts and feelings into alignment with what is true. Then you can get it on an inner level, which must be followed by attracting it on an outer level.

Keep this practice light and joyous. Have fun with it. Dr. Jean Houston once told me that we in Unity are too tame with our affirmations. We should dance them and chant them and dream them and do whatever we can to fully integrate them into our consciousness.

Get into them! Let them get into you! Then your affirmative prayer will align you with your highest good and bring this good forward into outer expression.

A prayer that David and I do throughout the day is one that we first learned from a spiritual healer and our friend, Dennis Adams: "I love you, God." We repeat this prayer numerous times during the day. Say this little prayer upon awakening and as the last thing before you drift off to sleep. You will be enfolded in grace throughout the day, and your sleep will be deep and peaceful. Affirming "I love you, God" throughout the day makes your entire day a prayer. Hold God in your heart and your love cannot be far behind. Hold the awareness of God's presence within your heart and you are already one with love. Remember, love attracts love.

A loving prayer to say first for yourself and then for others comes from the Buddhist tradition. It is to be slowly, mindfully repeated in the morning and whenever you have a quiet moment during the day. At day's end, it is to be thoughtfully repeated once again as you peacefully drift off to sleep. Here is this beautiful prayer:

May I be filled with loving kindness.
May I be well.
May I be peaceful and at ease.
May I be happy.

After reciting this for yourself for at least a month, you may wish to send this prayer to others:

May you be filled with loving kindness.
May you be well.
May you be peaceful and at ease.
May you be happy.

The faithful practice of this prayer can result in an abiding sense of peace, order, and well-being. It is a wonderful way to share a blessed thought with those you love or with one who is troubled.

Time and time again, I have seen miraculous answers to prayer. Prayer does change things in the outer. Talk to God as you talk to your dearest friend. Ask for help when help is needed. Affirm when you need to be reminded of who you truly are and who God is. Bless others with love when they are in need. And remember to give thanks when your prayers are answered or even before, knowing absolutely that they will be answered. Listen to the answer. Trust it and you will soon notice that your prayers are answered very quickly. Like anything else, the more we pay attention, the more we will recognize answers when they appear. This process opens doors and creates opportunities and healings that otherwise would not have occurred. We condition our whole lives with prayer by holding love within our hearts.

Meditation

Not better, but different from prayer, is meditation. I began meditating daily over twenty years ago. The whole idea of meditating just resonated with my soul.

In the seventies, my younger brother Jim and our minister were deeply involved in biofeedback meditation. At that time it was the latest thing in the consciousness arena. Jim had taught me to meditate and hooked me up to his biofeedback equipment. Very rapidly I would drop from the outer-directed state of mind, beta, into alpha, the centered consciousness, and in a minute or two would be deep into theta brain waves. I was able to do this in a classroom setting and was used to demonstrate meditation techniques at lectures and conference presentations. Meditation became very natural for me. It brought me a

calm and peace I hadn't known before. It was how I kept myself
at a functional level through times of turmoil and conflict.

If prayer is talking to God, meditation can be said to be the
time when God can talk back. Meditation is listening to God.

In meditation the idea is to clear your thoughts and thus
your mind so completely that you enter into a deeper realm of
being. For most people, this takes years of daily practice. On my
office wall, in front of my desk, is a blowup from a magazine ad
that says in very large letters, "In 28 minutes you'll be meditating like a Zen monk." Every time it catches my eye, I chuckle.
That's the American racing mentality. We want it and we want it
now. Zen monks meditate from four to eight hours a day, seven
days a week, for their entire lives. We are hardly going to attain
a similar state of awareness in twenty-eight minutes.

Meditation means taking the time to clear out the clutter
and center into your essence. It is like a healing balm gently
sliding over your soul. Meditation refreshes and renews your
mind and body. It will give you clear insight and direction and
bring vitality and radiance to you as well. People who meditate
regularly develop a glow that is unmistakable.

In the autumn of 1991, H.H. the Dalai Lama was in New
York City presenting an eight-day program that I was blessed to
attend. As His Holiness was speaking on meditation, he advised
those in attendance that we needed to spend four hours a day
in meditation. Four hours! You could hear the crowd gasp.

Well, I must admit I have never gotten up to four, but that
day I did make a commitment to do two hours a day. Up until
that time, my daily meditations were thirty to forty-five minutes
and I thought that was pretty good.

Now I do two hours a day by getting up very early in the
morning, usually by four-thirty or five, always by six, and in the
predawn I meditate for sixty to seventy-five minutes. At another

time during the day, or in the early evening, I will meditate the remaining time, usually in one session, sometimes in two.

What I have gained by these extended meditations is the movement into levels of consciousness that before this commitment I had not even imagined. It is precious time to me. It feeds my soul and nourishes my spirit. I cannot emphasize enough that I see daily meditation as the single greatest thing you can do for yourself. Meditation allows you to focus in on what is valuable and worthy of your time and attention. The rest is not valuable and needs to be let go. In this world, so much of our time is filled with drivel. Don't allow your ego to convince you that you haven't the time to pray and meditate.

When I was a young married woman, the first car that was actually mine was a little Triumph. I lived in Virginia Beach and used to tool around with the windows down and my hair blowing in the wind. I thought I was pretty hot stuff. My foot was made of lead and I was always in a hurry. One afternoon I came to a screeching halt, nearly plowing into the car stopped at a light in front of me. As I impatiently sat there, I read the bumper sticker staring at me: "If you're too busy to pray, you're too busy."

That little bumper sticker changed my life. It was one of those cosmic wake-up calls. I started to slow down, not only my driving, but my life.

Maybe you still think that you are too busy. Check out how many hours a day you watch TV, chat on the phone about nothing, or engage in gossip or mindless activity. We all have the time, but not all of us choose to use our time to connect with our essence. If you are new to meditation, I do not suggest that you attempt to tackle four hours. Fifteen minutes twice a day makes an excellent starting place.

Through the ages it has been taught that the still, pre-dawn hours are the best time to meditate. The reason for this is not hard to find: the busy activity of the day has not begun; the energy of the earth is quiet. If you can't bear the thought of getting up so early, pick another time when you can remain undisturbed for twenty minutes. An unfamiliar meditation tape or CD, played softly, can be helpful.

Sit on a chair or on the floor. If you stay in bed, you greatly increase the chances of going back to sleep. If you choose a chair, plant your feet on the floor, and whether you are in a chair or on the floor, keep your spine straight yet relaxed, and gently close your eyes.

Take several long, deep, slow breaths, giving particular attention to the exhalation. This will help you let go, release, and relax. Most adults need to relearn how to breathe. Many of us have become shallow, upper-chest breathers, using only a small portion of our lung capacity.

After the deep-breathing exercise, begin to relax your body, starting at your head and ending at the soles of your feet. Take a full, deep breath in and visualize it filling your head, your brain, and your brow. Exhale and think: *Relax*. Then consciously release the tension you have held in and around your head. Do this several times and then move down to your neck.

Breathe deeply, and slowly lower the right side of your head until your right ear reaches or nears your right shoulder. Breathe. Think: *Relax*. Feel the tension ooze out. Repeat as you lower the left side of your head to your left shoulder. Breathe. Continue moving this increasing sense of release and relaxation downward through your shoulder. Breathe. Move down the spine, flowing across the back and through the chest cavity. Imagine you are relaxing your inner organs. As you come to each set of muscles, tighten them for three seconds, then totally relax them.

Continue with the deep breathing and relaxing technique as you move down the body, through the legs and feet, concluding by releasing all tension out the soles of your feet. Let all stress, strain, and tension flow out of you during this meditative process. After you are thoroughly relaxed, just observe your thoughts and to each one affirm, "Peace be still." Do this until you feel very quiet.

See if you can simply be for several minutes, without any thoughts intruding upon your peace. As you become more accustomed to sitting still and moving into a meditative state, this period without thought will naturally become longer.

Another meditation technique is to choose one affirmation and use it as a mantra to lead you into and out of the meditative state. Start with one of the short, simple affirmations, such as "I am peace."

Again, find a comfortable position in a place where you will be undisturbed. Close your eyes, inhale deeply, and exhale slowly and completely. After several repetitions of this deep breathing, silently affirm on the inhalation, "I am," then just be still and into that affirmation for a moment. Then slowly exhale and silently affirm, "Peace."

Inhale: "I am."

Exhale: "Peace."

Move deeper into the quiet.

Inhale: "I am."

Exhale: "Peace."

Continue these repetitions as long as you remain focused totally on them. With practice, you will be able to use this process to lead you into a meditative state where you can remain as long as you wish. Then, when you sense it is time to return from the meditative state, begin the deep breathing again with "I am" on the inhalation and "Peace" on the exhalation. Allow the renewed repeating of the affirmation to gently lift you out of the meditation. When you feel complete, slowly open your eyes and go into your day centered, peaceful, and clear.

This is just a simple beginning. There are many excellent teachers, books, and programs on meditation. As you move more into the practice and begin gaining the benefits, you may want to take a class on meditation or study more thoroughly on your own. You could contact a Unity church in your area to see what meditation sessions or classes they offer.

Through visualization, prayer, and meditation, you are refining your vibration. You are bringing yourself into closer harmony with the ever-constant flow of universal oneness.

Not only do these practices bring you closer to God, they also bring you inner peace, tranquillity, and a certainty about all of life. These are definitely attributes that make you an attractive person and a highly desirable one. These practices bring to your awareness your holiness; they heal your relationship with God.

Investing in these practices will mean committing a chunk of your time daily to your spiritual life. It will mean being more disciplined than you probably have been. And it will mean you will be on the receiving end of yet-to-be-imagined blessings. Your soul is being healed.

Make the investment in yourself and miracles will become natural for you and love will enfold you.

⚛ 10 ⚛

Rising in Love

I share with you now the message of my heart. My prayer is that it connects with that place in your heart where we share the "knowing."

Rising in love is a lesson I know a great deal about because of *falling in love* so many times. Listen, hear those words: falling in love. What kind of imagery does "falling" conjure up for you? Why is it that we associate love with falling? Is there indeed a level of our being where we have always known that falling is not the direction to go with love? Falling into being less than you are so that your partner can be inflated. Falling in consciousness. Falling into dysfunctional behavior. Falling into pain and suffering. Falling into your life not working.

In my times of "falling in love," I believed that if I could just work hard enough, sacrifice myself more, it would work out, it would feel like love. How many times have you done that as well? How many times have you fallen into a special, unholy relationship and called it love? We create these supposedly "loving" relationships and there is everything but love in them.

The words *falling in love* have such romantic connotations. The poet writes verse to its mystery; the artist blends paint on canvas to capture the sensation; the songwriter composes lyrics praising its joys—and its pain. I ask you to hear these words as if they are being spoken for the very first time: *falling in love.* Perhaps what we are actually saying is not that you are falling in love, but that you are dropping in consciousness. You are dropping into pretending and settling. You are dropping into sacrificing parts of yourself in an attempt to make the relationship work.

I strongly believe we need to transform our language, concepts, and consciousness with regard to love. When we subconsciously tell ourselves that we're falling in love, the whole experience is doomed to fail. Whenever we give up a part of ourselves in our attempt to cling to love, we feel not only cheated but angry and guilty as well. As the initial bloom begins to fade and we catch a glimpse of what we're blindly walking into again, the Play button on our inner recorder gets pushed and we start an inner chant that goes something like this: "I've done it again, I've done it again," or "Love will never work for me." And on we go. The negative statement becomes our mantra, as we chant it over and over again.

The Sufis have a name for such an inner chant. It's called a *zikr* (pronounced "zicker"). Now a *zikr* is a *positive* tool of repetition to awaken us into deeper levels of consciousness and come into union with our beloved. We have created what I call a "negative *zikr*," on which our inner dialogue gets stuck: "I'll never make it. I'll never be happy. This kind of thing always happens to me. I'm too old." This last one I repeated to myself when I was barely over thirty!

These negative *zikr*s are anything but loving and supportive. They are a way to continue internalizing the pain and beat yourself up even more. They keep you stuck in an old pattern by constantly reinforcing it. Consider what kind of negative *zikr* you have been running inside your head in regard to relationships: *No one understands me. I'll never find what I desire. It's too late for me. Any attention is better than none.*

What have your chants been? Write them down as they come to you, and later in this chapter I'll give you an exercise to exorcise them.

Sufism teaches a very different and beautiful concept of love. The Sufis see love not as something you fall into, but rather as that which your soul rises into. In that rising there is such a joining of the loved with the Beloved that the everyday restrictions and barriers to love's entrance become as nothing, as clouds that are easily permeated by the radiance of love's presence. The Sufis speak of and experience a joining that is seldom found in our Western literature or tradition.

The Sufi tradition teaches that pure bliss can be attained in this holy union with the Beloved of the Soul. The Beloved could be translated as the Christ of Christian metaphysics — not Jesus in your soul, but you carrying the same divine seed that He carried, and rising up in consciousness to such a height that you then can enter into a holy union with your Beloved. Meeting the Beloved of the Soul moves love out of the realm of possibility into a connection, a knowing, a quickening of your heart that is at once astounding, enticing, and divine. The Beloved brings to your awareness not what is, but what could be. The Beloved is the God part of you that has been waiting patiently for you to wake up, to acknowledge his or her presence, and to rise into this divine embrace.

Discovering the Beloved that has always been there is an encounter not of this world. You have to experience it firsthand to believe how incredible this union is. The Beloved of the Soul is there within you, has always been with you, will never leave you, knows who you are in all your glory, supports you in becoming the full expression of your inner essence, and delights in your doing so.

Your Beloved is waiting for you now to teach you the mysteries of the heart. To contact the Beloved, you must shift your focus off the negative *zikr* and turn your attention upward.

Exorcising the Negative Zikr

Let us now take a deeper look at what your negative *zikr* has been in regard to relationships. Get a pad of paper and a pencil or pen. Sit quietly, turn your attention inward, and listen to your chant. Write out those negative statements, one to a page.

Now what we are going to do with those statements is to reword them, turning each old negative statement into a new positive statement or affirmation. Then you will work with the affirmation until you absolutely know from your soul to your toes that it is true.

Here are examples of negative *zikr*s you may have chanted that wreaked havoc in your personal and professional life: *It's too late. I'm too old. Nothing ever works out for me. What can you expect?*

Let's take these and transform them into positive statements or affirmations:

"It's too late . . . It's too late . . . It's too late," on and on goes your chant, which we now transform into: "The timing in my life is always perfect." "What can you expect?" transforms into "I expect and get only the best."

Believe me, when you first write those affirmations, you (1) probably will not believe them and (2) will think they are ridiculous. I certainly did. But I had been told that this would help me get off the roller coaster of failed relationships, so I was willing to give it a try. I hope you are willing as well.

As you continue to clear out on deeper and deeper levels, the negative *zikr* ceases its chant. Then you can begin to reinforce the truth of the transformative thought by affirming or chanting it again and again. Doing so brings the knowing of its truth and wisdom from your soul into your actual experience. It spirals you up one more level in your rising into love.

The great twelfth-century Sufi poet and mystic named Rumi knew the wonders of union with the Beloved. He wrote extensively on this meeting with the Beloved and the ecstasy it brings:

> *The minute I heard my first love story*
> *I started looking for you, not knowing how blind I was.*
>
> *Lovers don't finally meet somewhere.*
> *They're in each other all along.*
>
> *During the day I was singing with you.*
> *At night we slept in the same bed.*
> *I wasn't conscious day or night.*
> *I thought I knew who I was, but I was you.*

As you clear out the negative *zikr*s, you can begin to rise in love to meet the Beloved of the Soul. You will then always remain aware of love's presence. The support of the Beloved will be with you always. You will never feel alone again.

The Beloved knows your perfection, beholds you as God created you, and always sees through the flaws to your inner perfection. He or she supports you in knowing yourself as the Beloved knows you. It is not too much to ask of life to support you on this level. Anything less is asking for and accepting too little. You don't ask too much of life, but far too little.

You, too, can catch the higher vision, rise up in love, never again to fall into being less than you truly are, never again falling into a special relationship, but rising into a holy one. When you look within and find the Beloved of your Soul, you have truly discovered love's presence.

Rising to meet the Beloved is a way to know love without the body's interference. It is a way of bypassing the ego. You are—have always been—host to the Beloved, and your lovely guest is waiting patiently for your welcome. In your act of rising up, in those same moments, the essence of the Beloved is drawn into your heart and Love is drawn unto itself.

Meeting the Beloved means knowing love completely. Once you know love completely, you can never again be satisfied with specialness or stay for long in an unholy relationship. When you know love so completely, there is the natural desire to extend love and share with another on this profound level of bliss. When you know it yourself, within yourself, then you can give it away. You can give out of your fullness, rather than attempting to give out of your emptiness and only further depleting your storehouse. Now you are a holy person, no longer a person filled with holes.

Giving until there is nothing left is not holy—it is madness. Love never asks for sacrifice, but the ego always does. If you believe that sacrifice is love, then you must learn that sacrifice is actually separation from love. Our confusion of sacrifice with love has been so profound that we cannot conceive of love without sacrifice. As we rise in love, so does our understanding of what love is. Only then can we truly come to know that sacrifice is attack and not love. Sacrifice within a relationship, your sacrifice or your partner's, is really an attempt to control the other person. "After all I've done for you, given up for you, and now you _____." I know you can fill in the blank. You've probably heard it before, thought it, maybe even said it.

When you love out of your fullness, you do not have to be less so that the other person can be more. Each one gets to be a radiant, shining light, thus increasing the magnitude of both.

An old *New Yorker* cartoon that I clipped and saved depicts two women meeting on a city street corner. The first woman says to the second, "My gosh, Gladys, you haven't changed in more than forty years!" And Gladys hadn't changed. She looked like she had stepped right out of a World War II movie. She looked like a 1944 special with her rolled hair, platform shoes, and huge eyebrows. To be told you haven't changed in forty years, or in twenty, or in ten is *not* a compliment. Love changes you. Love releases your inner beauty. Love calls forth your inner magnificence and it shines through. Until you know love truly, for yourself, it cannot be seen by or shared with others. Once you know love, it cannot be contained.

As you rise in love, you come to love life so completely that others are naturally drawn to you, delight in being with you. It's as if you've discovered a wonderful, long-hidden secret and now you get to tell the world of its blessings. Everyone wants to know what it is. The stars literally begin to move for you as you rise to a new and yet ancient understanding of love.

We must transform our concept of being in love from falling to rising, allowing love not only to fill us but to lift us to new heights of ecstasy and bliss. When we rise in love, our entire energy field—body, soul, and spirit—ascends to enter into holy union with the Beloved.

This radical shift from falling to rising begins to take place when we recognize where we have been so often with regard to love—in the pits! We can then begin to transform our perceptions, no longer seeing love as something that happens to us, that we stumble into, but coming to view love as what we already are. This love is ever flowing within us and through us, and we each have the power to direct the flow upward.

There are many techniques to prepare your heart to awaken to such depths. One that can be easily practiced on your own comes out of the Sufi tradition, which I learned while studying with Dr. Jean Houston. Sit in a comfortable position with your spine straight and place an empty chair in front of you. Play a tape of soft, meditative music. My favorite for this exercise is *Fairy Ring* by Mike Rowland.

Most of us have learned how to build a fortress around our hearts. This technique, which is the proper use of a *zikr*, allows us to relax and permits the fortress walls to crumble. When done properly, this *zikr* leads one into holy union with the Divine Lover or the Beloved. It is a remarkable experience.

You will need a way to keep count of thirty-three exhalations. You may use a rosary if you have one. I have found that fingers work just as well; you just have to focus a little more. What you are going to do during this exercise is take thirty-three very deep breaths and visualize the breath penetrating your heart center (in the middle of your chest, just to the right of your heart). With each exhalation, you will make the deep resonating sound of "hmmmmm" three times. Also, you gently tap your heart center several times on each exhalation.

Inhale slowly and fully, and exhale to the sound of "hmmmmm, hmmmmm, hmmmmm," as you tap your chest three or more times. Repeat the cycle thirty-three times. As you progress, you may experience a buzzing sensation in your head, chest, or body. Do not be frightened. This is very good. The energy is beginning to be quickened and to flow. Take your time during the thirty-three repetitions. When you have finished, sit silently and envision the Beloved coming to you through the call of this spiritual practice. Invite the Beloved now to sit before you in the available empty seat.

Your heart is now open, and you can with ease send love from your heart into the heart of the Beloved. In the same moment, you can visualize the Beloved sending his or her love into your heart. Be very still during this part and you will feel the sweetness of divine, holy love.

This may take several practices, until you fully realize the bliss available to each of us. Once you do, *falling* in love will never again be the direction you travel when you experience love. For now you know the mystery of the heart, and the only way to go is up.

Rumi wrote, "Love is not just the thirsty seeking the water, but the water seeking the thirsty." That which you seek is seeking you as well. What you have been seeking all along is love. All the while, love in its wonder has been seeking you. Rise now into the ideal. Rise into the possible. Rise in consciousness. Rise into the realization of love and come to love yourself and your new life with the Beloved.

When I was studying with Dr. Jean Houston, whose mentor had been Margaret Meade, she would tell the story of Dr. Meade's visits to her home. It seemed that a party was always going on wherever Margaret Meade was, even if she was the only person in the room. She had a most unusual morning ritual. She would get up before anyone else in the house had stirred and, upon rising from her bed, would stomp one foot and then the other on the floor, loudly. Then, at the top of her enormous voice, she would shout, "Thank God, I'm Margaret Meade!" And thus the entire household was awakened each morning.

Often at workshops, I'll have the participants reenact this ritual using their own names. On several occasions, folks have gotten so into it that they yell, "Thank God, I'm Margaret Meade." "No, no, you are you!" I'd shout back.

Do this exercise now if you like, or better still, when your feet hit the floor in the morning. Shout out, "Thank God, I'm _____." If you can do it with feeling and joy and really mean it, you have spiraled up one more level in rising in love. Margaret Meade obviously loved her life and her work. You can experience the same and even more. I thank God you are you, now rising in love.

The Beloved of the Soul with Skin On

"Okay, God, what I want now is to meet the Beloved of the Soul with Skin On." We learn how to recognize our problems. We learn how to forgive, to move out of specialness into holiness. We learn how to love ourselves and others unconditionally. Then we learn how to rise in love. We come to meet the Beloved, and still we want more. Yes! To meet our divine counterpart is a desire most of us carry.

The holy relationship is one of the ways God changes our dreams of fear to happy dreams. Happy dreams come true, not because they are dreams but because they are true.

Spiritual reality is to love your brother and sister as yourself. In a holy relationship, we have first learned to truly love ourselves and to then love our partner as we love ourselves. This is a blessed activity.

The reason we are here on this planet, going through our individual lives, is to love one another. The holy relationship is the means by which we do so. Our souls know this, and our souls have been orchestrating this meeting with our Beloved with Skin On. But it has taken us so long to quit screwing up the plan! We need to relinquish our itty-bitty plan for God's magnificent one. Step aside and allow God to come through. A great and simple prayer to keep in mind is, "I will step aside and let Him lead the way" (or you may want to say Her).

God is already leading you to your Beloved with Skin On, your soulmate; the one with whom you can share your life in love, honor, respect, and joy; the one with whom you can have fun, think in accord, and live in peace and harmony and love.

It is possible. Ask your soul. Listen to the wisdom, the knowing, that comes from within. If it speaks of love, unconditionally, it is from God. If it speaks of fear and separation and conditional caring, the ego has returned.

We make everything that should be natural and easy for us not only hard and difficult, but nearly impossible. Let's begin to allow it to be. Allow yourself to open to God's wondrous plan. Allow yourself to be happy. Know that you are deserving. It is right to make manifest what you know in your soul is possible. This is the ideal that you can obtain, whether you are currently in a relationship or not.

If you are in a relationship and do truly care for your partner and want your relationship to continue, begin right now to treat your partner like the precious treasure of God that he or she is. How would you treat a newborn infant? How would you treat the president and the first lady if they came to your home for dinner, or Julia Child if you were invited to lunch with her, or H.H. the Dalai Lama if you were invited to meditate with him?

How would you treat these people? Is it better than you are treating your partner right now? If so, ask yourself why that is. Why would you extend more care and graciousness to a stranger than to your spouse or partner? We do that—and when we get off autopilot and look at our behavior, it is pretty strange. Treat the one you are with as if he or she is the most valued treasure on the planet and you will be astounded at how your partner, the relationship, and you will change.

I knew a couple who had been married for a number of years and lived in a relationship filled with much ego activity. The flame of their love had diminished to a faint ember. For their thirtieth anniversary, their children gave them a trip to Hawaii, where they were heard making an agreement with each other while sitting on the beach: "The beauty of this place moves me so, let's agree to put down our weapons while we are here and *pretend* we are in love." Do that with your current significant other and see what happens. It changed the lives of that couple.

They rekindled that spark of love they had held for each other long ago. They spoke kindly to each other. They listened to each other. They enjoyed activities together and gave each other space to pursue their own interests. One day he went deep-sea fishing while she enjoyed the day playing bridge with new friends. They had a wonderful vacation, saw once again what had originally attracted each to the other, and returned home resolved to stay in this loving space.

You cannot love another unconditionally without some very dynamic changes occurring, and those changes won't be just in the other person. Whatever is going on in your relationship right now, ask yourself, "How can I be more loving?" Your answer from the Holy Spirit will never be: withhold. It will always be: bless; flood your consciousness and the other's with compassion, kindness, and love, unconditional love. To forgive, to love unconditionally, is always the way to go. When we can truly practice unconditional love, everyone is blessed, even in the cases where the relationship ends.

If you are currently in a special and unholy relationship that does not appear to have any hope of being transformed into a holy one, and you realize it is best to part, you will be free only if all your actions around parting are taken in love. If you act out of anger, fear, or revenge, remember that consciousness will soon re-create itself. Do all that you need to do in love; desire the best for yourself and your partner. In love, free him or her to live out the soul's purpose. Desire only the best for your former partner and you will be free. Desire revenge and it is yourself you imprison. Release in love and you will open the way for your good to move forward and meet you.

A dear friend, Rachael, was going through a long and difficult divorce. There was an ocean of emotion to deal with. Sometimes when she called, she would be so upset that she wanted to kill her estranged husband or, possibly worse, emasculate him. She would rant and I would be very quiet. She would pause and start up again, and when she was finished, I would say, "He is your teacher. This is a hard lesson for you to get, so God sent you an excellent teacher. Love Clark, bless him, and let him go. Learn to love him in a divine, unconditional sort of way, a way that is unattached to outcome, and you'll be free."

She carried a great deal of sorrow and pain from a previous divorce, where the judge had divided the custody of her two daughters between herself and the former husband. A great deal of forgiveness still needed to be done with regard to that divorce and settlement. Rachael was fearful of repeating her history, this time having two sons from the marriage. The father was asking for primary custody of both boys, and my friend was filled with fear and outrage.

Now, many people would cry out, How awful, what an injustice! What is happening in the outer is never the issue, however. What is happening in the outer is a projection of what is happening within. Work on the inner projector and the outer projection will change.

We are, for the most part, like the old cowhand years ago who went to see his first motion picture. It was—what else?—a western. When the Indians began attacking the cavalry, the old cowboy stood up in the theater, drew his six-shooter, and started firing at the screen.

My friend's desire to turn her husband into a eunuch is like firing shots at the screen. When we don't like the outer projection of our lives, we are not to shoot the leading man or the bit players. We are to go within and fix the script of our minds.

Well, Rachael had tried not speaking to Clark, locking herself in a spare bedroom, ignoring him, hating him, and everything else—with no success. She finally tired of it all and became willing to lay her anger and grievances aside. So she went on a love-and-release campaign. She called one night, upset again, saying loving was working so well he wanted to make love with her and see if they could work through their differences. "So do you want to do that?" I asked. "No, I really don't." "Well, then tell him no." What had happened was that Clark had misread her energy and signals and translated them the only way he knew how.

She kept loving him, and their divorce went through without a wrinkle. She got custody of the boys and their dad got them two weekends a month and in the summers. She also kept their home, and they each got their freedom and an equitable division of property. Once she started loving, they quit slicing each other up and the situation worked out best for all concerned.

Love clears the way, opens doors that have been shut, and brings us untold blessings. It attracts, whereas fear and hatred bind us to their dreadful energies. If Rachael had left her marriage hating Clark, I am absolutely certain she would have created another special relationship, which very quickly would have looked exactly like her previous marriages.

When we heal the past through love, we are then free to create a future different from our past. Most of us carry that knowing that our perfect counterpart exists. I waited for my soulmate and husband for a long time, and I knew he was there.

Perhaps one reason so many people go through a number of marriages and partners is not only that they are looking for love outside themselves, but also that they are looking for their Beloved and just don't know how to go about it. The result is a succession of failed relationships . . . and the search goes on.

I certainly was expecting David before we met, and I was positive that we would recognize each other. I was so certain that this knowing would communicate "This is it—he's the one" that I quit dating and took myself off that emotional roller coaster. Giving yourself a respite from dating while doing your inner healing work can be most helpful. As you begin to feel healed and whole and less needy, then you can resume dating and attract healthy, nurturing, loving relationships.

Until my soulmate and I met, I was happy and complete within my life. It is such emotional freedom to experience your own completion, to have arrived at the place of being able to care for your own needs and still desire a partner. That desire comes now not out of a sense of incompletion or neediness. Rather, it is a desire to join with a partner in celebrating wholeness where both can truly love and support each other. I was no longer willing to share my spiritual, emotional, and soul essence with just a nice man. It had to be the *right* man.

I was ready to meet the Beloved with Skin On.

Soulmates Now Meeting at Gate 42

"You'll meet your soulmate when you least expect it," my life-long friend Ginna told me. Ha; I laughed at that notion.

"That's impossible. I expect him every single second of my life!" I exclaimed.

In June of 1986, Ginna, who lives in California, called and asked me to join her in Washington, D.C., over the Fourth of July weekend to attend a big Washington-style party. It was to be held at her brother's penthouse and I thought, well, why not. Life as a nondating single was fairly bleak in the party department, especially parties as festive as this one promised to be. Ginna and I always have a great time together, so off I went. This was very uncharacteristic of me to fly to another city for a party. Something outrageous was happening. It was exciting to be going away. Maybe I would meet my soulmate over the weekend.

Ginna's family treated me like a treasure and were most gracious in giving me my own little suite in their home. It had everything, including my own bathroom and scale.

Well, my size 8 slacks no longer fit, but when I stood on that scale, weighing myself for the first time in about three years, it was an icy shock. I weighed thirty pounds more than I had been telling myself. We may not be our bodies, but mine had pudged out and I was beyond upset. Even in my panic, I had this inner knowing that I was to go to Diet Center. Now, I knew nothing about Diet Center: I didn't know anyone who had gone there and I knew nothing of its program. But alongside my panic was this incredibly strong knowing about, of all things, Diet Center.

I flew home in time to lead the church service Sunday morning absolutely knowing I was going to Diet Center on Monday. I made the call I knew I would make, and the representative suggested I go to a newly opened center near the church. I was to be sure and ask for Sandy. She told me that Sandy was wonderful and would really help me. She assured me that everything was going to be okay. An appointment with Sandy was set for later that day. When I arrived at the designated hour, Sandy was busy with another client. I was given forms to fill out and again was assured that Sandy was wonderful. I was just going to love her.

A short while later Sandy arrived, warmly greeted me, and began reading the forms I had completed. She came to an abrupt stop, darted a piercing look at me, glanced at the forms again, and loudly exclaimed, "I know you!" To myself I silently responded, "Oh, shit!" I had wanted to go there anonymously, lose my chubs, and leave. But no, against all the odds, this woman knew me. At this point Sandy interrupted my thoughts with, "I was at your church yesterday for the first time."

Great, now I have a potential Unity member monitoring my progress. Bubbling with enthusiasm, Sandy led me into a tiny room and asked me to disrobe so that my weight and measurements could be taken. There I stood in my underwear with this stranger who had heard me deliver a Sunday lesson taking my measurements. As a matter of fact, she was taking my thigh measurements (which was not exactly thrilling me) when she said, "May I ask you a personal question?"

"My God, Sandy, I'm in my bikinis and you're measuring my thigh. How much more personal can we get?" Undaunted, she charged ahead.

"Are you single?" she inquired.

"Yes, I am," I responded.

In the next couple of seconds, the new path of my life began to unfold. Sandy began, "I know the most wonderful man that I know would love to meet you." My heart leapt.

"Tell me about him," I managed to croak.

"He's on the board of directors at my Unity church in Evanston, Illinois, and in my Arnold Patent support group. He's lived and worked around the world and is highly intelligent. He's a Scorpio [I am too], a vegetarian [I am too], very funny and fun to be with. He's pleasant looking, has been divorced for a number of years, and has three lovely grown daughters. He is also very kind and loving and successful in his career. All the single women at church are chasing him around the building, but he wants nothing to do with them."

I want you to really get this scene fixed in your mind. There I am standing in my underwear, chills of knowing running all over my body. My heart energy is exploding, and Sandy concludes by saying, "He's quit dating and gone home to pray for his soulmate." She points her index finger right at me and declares, "I think you're it."

Every cell in my being was charged with electrical current. For the first time I knew what it meant in the Bible where it says, "Mary's heart leapt." Mine felt like it was about to explode.

I knew Sandy was speaking of the man I had been seeking. "Give this man my phone number!" I cried. She immediately called David and found out he was in California at a retreat. Fabulous! A man who travels across the country to go on a retreat is my kind of man.

When David returned home, he found an urgent message from Sandy on his answering machine: "David, you've got to call me immediately. I've found your soulmate!" David, a good friend of Sandy's, thought she had lost it. But he was intrigued, so he called her.

He then proceeded to call me and left a message on my answering machine saying he was Sandy's friend from Chicago and would call back later that evening, but if I came home and wanted to call, here were the phone numbers. His voice sounded wonderful on the tape, and I began to think that maybe this man has used all his gumption to call this unknown woman in Cleveland. Maybe he wouldn't feel comfortable enough to call a second time. I could call him (which would be very out of character for me), but first I would sit down and meditate and pray about it.

I sat down, put myself in a meditative posture, closed my eyes . . . and the phone rang. It was David. We talked for an hour and a half, and there was a comfortable familiarity, an instant connection. We spoke every other night over a span of ten days. We were talking from our hearts, sharing our ideals with each other, getting to know each other without our bodies and sex being an issue.

He made plans to fly in from Chicago the next Friday for a blind date. On the appointed day I left the office early to go home and freshen up before going to the airport. Waiting for me were a dozen red and yellow roses from David. The card read, "To the joy of discovery." If this man was trying to impress me, he was doing a good job.

When we actually met at the airport, there was on both our parts an instant recognition of our essence and not a recognition of our physical beings. It was a very odd sensation. David came in on Friday and ended up staying until Tuesday. He came back to Cleveland again on Friday of the same week. After that, we spent every weekend together, except when I had a commitment to be out of the country for two weeks. We were married eight months later.

My father, out of concern and certainly aware of my history, questioned me as to whether we were moving too fast. "Dad, this one I know. I don't know because of our time together, but because my soul knows this man," I told him. Every level of my being recognized and knew David. And he knew me. He freely tells people he knew he was going to marry me before we ever met at gate 42.

My friend Ginna was right, because it did happen when I least expected it, while Sandy was taking my thigh measurement. David and I were drawn together across time and space. Our recognition of our souls' qualities was there from our first contact.

Soulmates are just that—souls who are mated. Not two half beings, but two whole, complete beings coming together. When two individuals try to become one, they are decreasing their magnitude. Here again is a concept that departs radically from the world's teaching. We truly must be willing to question every value we hold and explore for ourselves what is really true.

If you've held the idea that finding a soulmate would complete you, give it up. Be complete within yourself and then you can join with your soulmate not out of emptiness, but to support you in knowing your fullness.

Meeting David was the culmination of years of preparation and purification. As I said to him during our first weekend together, "You were worth the wait," and "Of all my great manifestations, you are the greatest."

Being with my soulmate is not work. Special relationships need work and need it constantly. Holy relationships are not work. They simply are. In a holy relationship, each one has looked within and sees no lack. We have healed those places in us that were bruised or saddened. Our being together is joy. We have put the God part of us first, and everything else naturally falls into its perfect place. David and I loved each other before we actually met in this life's experience. Our personal interests are very similar and where they differ, we respect the other. I feel so totally loved by this gift God has sent. On days when I think I look dreadful, he sees only beauty. His love is not based on how I look or act, or on what I say or do. It is just there, no matter what. It is like a granite foundation, solid, unshakable, eternal.

Soulmates do recognize each other. There is an instant familiarity, a repose, as if you have always been together. It is being totally comfortable with another person. It is loving that one as yourself.

On one level we are all one, but we have lost sight of our oneness. A holy relationship with a soulmate restores our sight in a holy instant. Here we are given a glimpse of eternity. For in our awareness of oneness with our beloved, our love comes closest to God's. We can see our sameness, rather than focusing on our separateness. Now we can move into our true identity. We are given a glimpse of heaven and see our partner as God's holy son or daughter. Life becomes a treasure house filled with rich and limitless gifts. It is here that you see your partner's holiness in every instant and remember your own. In a holy relationship with a soulmate, we can remember who we truly are. Life is easy. It is a joy. The world's teaching is that life is difficult at best. The world asserts that you have to work at relationships and work hard if they are to be successful. The spiritual perspective is that in a holy relationship you never have to work on the relationship, only on yourself.

This takes a quantum shift in understanding, but in order to live the joy-filled lives that are possible, we must make the shift. We work on ourselves, not on the relationship. When we insist that it is the relationship we must work on, we are putting the focus for healing where healing can never be attained. We become like the cowboy shooting at the picture screen.

In a relationship with our soulmate, we close the gap and can experience our oneness. What we feel and acknowledge in this one is what someday we will behold in all. Being with a soulmate shows us a world beyond the body until the body is seen as but a haze encircling the wonder of your beloved. It is not your beloved but only an image of him or her. When we can see beyond the sight our eyes show us, then we can see our loved one as so much more than just his or her physical self and behold ourselves in that knowing as well. We come to see our beloved's holiness and innocence, and our own as well, in a holy relationship with our soulmate.

Living with a soulmate, you have the opportunity to cease judging yourself, which means you will not be judging your partner. You will only be loving him or her in a divine uniting.

There is no projection of guilt or fear when each remembers his or her innocence and divinity.

Soulmates in healed relationships are fun, easy, joyful, and holy. They attest to what we always knew was possible. They are limitless in their ability to bless each other and everyone they meet, whether that meeting lasts for an instant or a lifetime. In this holy union the possibility is given to live a sacred life, to rise out of the illusion, the appearance of what life is, and into its divine reality. Of course there will be times when judgment, criticism, and unforgiveness tempt you, but now you know you have the means to escape that ancient model that separates. You return to how life can be experienced when free from thoughts of separation.

As Leslie Parrish remarks in her husband Richard Bach's book *A Bridge Across Forever,* "A soulmate is someone who has locks that fit our keys, and keys to fit our locks." When we find the lock, we know it. It can be a perfect fit if we are willing to release our old grievances and negative patterns and allow Divine Love to direct the relationship.

Encounters with a soulmate do not necessarily last a lifetime. You may have experiences with a soulmate that are brief and perhaps not intimate. Your missions may not be taking the same course in this life experience, but in the time you spend together there is a recognition, admiration, and love that transcends the body. People have shared many soulmate encounters with me. Some were instant and eternal. Others were brief and casual and yet filled with an immediate depth and openness.

A soulmate encounter may occur between two people of extremely dissimilar ages. I believe this can explain the reported romances between, for example, a mature, perhaps even matronly, woman and a far younger man. People may question what he sees in her. He sees her soul and he remembers.

Such was the case with Anita and Todd. At the time of Anita's divorce, she was praying to meet her true soulmate and asked to be shown what he looked like so she might recognize him when they met. She was shown the image of a teenage boy whom she knew. Astonished and shocked, she protested that he couldn't be her soulmate. The message came back that in four years they would begin their relationship. In four years they did begin a relationship. He was a young man and she a mature woman. They have been together for seven years and are joyfully happy.

We may also witness soulmate encounters where the life circumstances and commitments of one or both do not allow them to be easily together. If they force their relationship, a great deal of pain and suffering can result.

Such was the case with Candy and Kevin. She was working on her Ph.D. and had never been married or in a serious relationship. Candy was quite intellectual by nature. Her responses to life were always totally rational until she met Kevin, fifteen years her senior. He had been married over twenty-five years to a woman with whom he professed to share no common interests or goals. The marriage was dead, according to Kevin. Kevin was an open, gentle, kind, caring man. Candy found herself incredibly drawn to him and, caught in the emotional pull, she would not rise above her longings for intimacy.

Kevin and Candy were remarkably attracted to each other, not just physically, but intellectually and emotionally. They walked to the beat of the same drummer. They were both advanced practitioners of yoga; both frequently attended week-long seminars and self-help workshops; both were highly intelligent, quiet, reflective people. They began having an affair while Kevin was still with his wife. Candy pleaded constantly for Kevin to give more to their relationship. He kept promising he would leave when his children were out of high school, after his daughter's wedding, after his mother-in-law recovered from an illness. Candy settled for crumbs and became increasingly angry with Kevin, with herself, and with life.

What very well could have been a soulmate connection, for they did love each other on a soul level, turned almost immediately into a special relationship filled with unmet promises, broken dates, lies, anxiety, and sorrow. What could have remained holy became an emotional addiction for which only now, fifteen years later, Candy has broken off and sought help.

We are not to bed down with everyone to whom we are attracted—even if we believe that one to be our soulmate. When we add a level of intimacy not intended for a specific relationship at that time, we can cause a great deal of suffering and escalating guilt for everyone. As my friend Christine says, "It makes you crazy." It is here that we fill up that nine-tenths of the iceberg that lies hidden beneath the surface.

"Only one" is a concept many of us carry. There is "only one" job opportunity and you lost it—your life's career is doomed. There is "only one" soulmate and he is taken—your love life is doomed. Nonsense! This is childish thinking. In this vast, rich, lavish universe, do you really believe God created only one possibility for you to know bliss? What if, instead of being thirty years your junior or senior (which could be challenging), your soulmate lived in the fourteenth century and you missed each other by six hundred years! "Only one" is a belief of the ego.

If you are clear in your intention and absolutely committed to living in a holy relationship with a soulmate, your sincere desire will be blessed. The Laws of Love do not withhold from us. We are the ones who think that withholding must be our job. It's nobody's job, so be certain you are no longer doing it to yourself.

Being in a relationship with your soulmate does not mean you exclude others from your love. Your heart is now open to welcome more people within the circle of your love. Love is not separation and exclusion. Love is healing and inclusion. It is truly in the presence of love that two individuals recognize each other and unite. To me, it is the most awesome gift that God gives us: to love with this depth and holiness.

Many Soulmates

We have many soulmates, not just one, which is the only way it could be if life is to make any sense. So if you lost what you thought was the "love of your life" through a move when you were a child or because of an existing marriage or even death, there is another one for you. If you have ever had a soulmate encounter, you can have another one.

Bless what was or what could have been that never was. Free yourself from that memory out of the past, no matter how lovely. Open your heart to your present good. Open your heart to recognize your soulmate now.

Perhaps you and your beloved have already met, but you did not recognize each other because your glasses were cloudy. Maybe even now, right beside you, sits your beloved and you have not recognized her or him because you decided how this person would look and be and then you asked for your beloved.

That is the reverse of how we are to ask and attract. Clear your mind of all your ideas of how this person will show up, and begin to treat everyone as you would want to be treated. When you do that, you will start to see the inner spirit in everyone. The love that you are giving out to all absolutely has to attract to you an equal expression of love. You and your soulmate will be drawn together across time and space. It doesn't matter if you live next door or a continent apart, love will draw you together.

Surrendering to Divine Love

If you are in a holy relationship, the greatest way I know to keep your love alive and growing ever deeper is to give God your relationship as a gift. Allow this Divine Love in every instant to lift from you anything and everything that would hurt you, and give to you everything that would continue to be a blessing unto your holiness and wholeness.

In the instant that a thought arises that would separate you from your ultimate good, allow Divine Love to take it and replace it with a loving, healing thought. Give to Divine Love, the power of Love within you, any thought of unworthiness, depression, shame, or guilt. Release sadness and anger, your judgments and criticisms of others and of yourself. Love knows that these thoughts are meaningless, but you do not.

When we ask the power of Divine Love to guide us and give love to our relationship, we will always be given a message that speaks for the right choice, helping us to remember to love. When we give any occurrence over to Divine Love, the answer comes quickly, surely, and with love for everyone. Many of us grew up with the concept of the body being a temple. Shift now in your thinking and see your holy relationship as the temple where Divine Love can truly dwell.

When any problem arises in the union between two soulmates, the problem need not be resolved by the couple alone. The problem should be given to the power of Love, which is greater than any conflict and where the disturbance can experience resolution. This resolution will always be perfect and complete. I have noticed through the years that Love's answers to our perceived problems are very seldom what we had conjured up, but infinitely more creative and long-lasting.

In the very act of surrendering to Divine Love, you both are exhibiting a willingness to be shown a better way. That better way is always the perfect answer where all get to be winners. One partner does not have to suffer loss in order for the other to gain.

Give your relationship to Divine Love to be used for a higher purpose, and you and your partner will be spared from ever living out of littleness. The purpose that Divine Love has for your relationship is so much more than any of us are ever able to conceive. This does call for faith and a relinquishment of control. Usually, by the time we arrive in a holy relationship, we have already realized that the whole notion of our controlling anything is pretty comical. *A Course in Miracles* says it would be like a sunbeam thinking it is the sun or a wave believing it can control the entire ocean.

To be truly happy we must one day make the decision to give our old, worn-out, tired relationship to Love to transform, heal, and use for a higher purpose. In turning the relationship over to God, we are agreeing to bring it into alignment with heaven's purpose, which is "to make happy." We are asking that our relationship be restored to sanity, selflessness, and love. We are willingly relinquishing the ego's purpose, which has been to fragment and separate. Surely this has not made anyone happy. No one can find happiness while attempting to make the partner feel guilty or looking for someone to blame for one's own current state of misery.

Once we recognize that our alliance has had unholiness as its purpose and once we desire to have it be another way, we can pray. In our prayers we ask the Spirit within to enter this ego-based, fear-filled picture. We simply give the relationship, with all its ego demands, ancient grievances, and perceived joys (for no relationship is without its moments of light), to the indwelling power of Love.

In that single act the entire course of the relationship is abruptly shifted from what the ego has created to what Love would have it be. It is here that we can begin to understand that maybe, just maybe, God has a better game plan than the one currently running. Perhaps God's will could be for our greatest good.

As spiritual beings having this human experience, we can certainly be the most curious of creatures. All of us have believed that we have a better idea than any higher power could ever have of what will work best in our lives. Who of us has not heard the words *the will of God* and been filled with fear and dread? Fear of the will of God is one of the strangest ideas the human mind has ever created. It isn't God's will we should be afraid of, but our own. Some tragedy happens, and what do we say but, "Ah, it was God's will." Something fabulous occurs and we say, "Ah, such luck!" Now tell me, is this not upside-down thinking? Fortunate events are ascribed to luck and unfortunate ones are God's will. I think not.

You may have to do some work on yourself to get over a fear of accepting God's will as only good. When we deny God's will, we are denying joy. God does not deny us our good, joy, and pleasure, but the ego always does. I like the way my friend, the respected author Wayne Dyer, so simply puts it, "Get it! God's will works! Yours doesn't!"

So we get uncomfortable enough to recognize that there must be another way. We call upon the presence of Divine

Love, which has always been available to us but does not intrude upon our free will. Love will enter only by invitation. That is, you must say, "God, please help me. I give you what I have made of this relationship, and I ask you to heal me and it to our depths." Or you can use the short route, "God, here's the mess I made. Do something with it." From that point on, the relationship will begin to shift, for it now has holiness as its newfound purpose.

Specialness can never be a satisfactory replacement for holiness. At this initial stage, the need for faith is strong, for the relationship may seem disturbed, disjointed, and even quite distressing. Many relationships have been broken off at this point and the old unholy pursuits taken up again, in yet another search for specialness.

Allow Love to be in charge and you will experience being with your soulmate as living together in constant trust that every detail of your lives is already handled. Arnold Patent teaches, "Let the universe handle the details." This is simply another way of saying the same thing. A code that I live by is, "Keep my appointment." I just show up where I have agreed to be and when. Then I let Divine Love handle the details of my life from there. This state of connection has taken years to attain, but I truly know that everything is always working out exactly as it needs to. God is in charge. Remember, God's plan works; yours doesn't. God's plan always works. David and I both understand that and live our lives by this principle.

Meeting your soulmate may be one of the first steps to living in a holy relationship blessed every instant by love, but it isn't the last step. Now the two of you can walk together hand-in-hand to God.

Holy Sex

Holy sex is not about technique or tantric positions. It is about how lovemaking between two who are soulmated is different from other merely physical unions. Holy sex is also about how this union can be exquisitely pleasurable not just to the body, but to the soul and spirit as well. It is about lights flashing around you, which is really your energy fields igniting, feeling a presence within the room, being aware of the energy within the chakras expanding. It is about a sense of wonder and gratitude, about touching a larger reality and entering there together for several sacred moments.

When the wounds of our past are healed and we are emotionally and spiritually clear, our sexual unions with the beloved become sacred acts between not only our bodies but our souls as well. Here we can release our imprisoned splendor and soar in ecstasy together. In such unions, our sexual energy becomes one with the creative force of the universe. In such blessed sexual unions, this energy can actually further heal each one. For many, their first total act of surrender occurs while making love with their soulmate.

Clear sexual energy is spiritual energy. Both come from the same source—God. To experience holy sex it is necessary to trust totally: to trust yourself; to trust your partner with your body, your vulnerability, your very soul. Here there is no longer a sense of having to do it "right," for all judgments have been dropped. Here you are safe to just be, without expectations, demands, or an agenda from your partner.

The ancient sacred text from China known as the Tao regards sex as one way to achieve enlightenment. I agree that our sexual expression can lead us into heightened states of awareness and into an expanded dimension of self. I have long considered our innate sexual drive to be about more than the propagation of our species. Every aspect of life has a spiritual dimension, and that certainly includes sex.

The early Taoists prescribed refraining from emission during intercourse in order to conserve the "sacred fluid." I have known a few who practiced the same discipline two thousand years later, but they did not appear to be particularly enlightened or even pleasing to be around. I believe we can glean much from this ancient knowledge without taking it 100 percent to heart or to the bedroom.

From the viewpoint of the unattached female, another aspect of holy sex needs to be mindfully considered. We as females are the receivers of the male, not only physically but emotionally and psychically as well. When a female has sexual relations with a male she barely knows or with whom she is not in accord, she is quite literally inviting the man's consciousness—with all its mixed thoughts and conflicting emotions—into her body and her auric field and psyche. This can be a very draining, disempowering experience. When done repeatedly without thought to the spiritual and soul effects, it can become a way in which women unconsciously devalue their worth.

The important point to remember is that the woman is the receiver, not just physiologically, but emotionally, spiritually, and psychically as well. Before going to bed with a new man, consider if you really want all of him, his neuroses, judgments, grievances, prejudices, likes and dislikes, ejaculated into you and into your essence.

I advise women to be mindful of who they are choosing to be intimate with. If you are focusing your time, energy, consciousness, and money on becoming a clear, forgiving, kind, and loving person, *do not* climb into bed with some hunk who is filled with unresolved conflict, anger, and hostility toward his mother or his former wife. When a conscious woman is intimate with a conflict-filled man, it can take months to get his energy out of her auric field. When you are working on being conscious and waking up, it is vitally important to have sexual relations only with one who is equally conscious and awake.

When a soulmated couple is quite clear emotionally, when both have resolved their individual soul issues, they can come together sexually in such a way that she, representing the female principle, and he, representing the male principle, unite equally, creating the condition for enlightenment. When we are unhealed and our wounds are oozing, this is not going to happen. When we are healed and our wounds transformed into vehicles of awakening, a remarkable energy is available to us that in other, previous circumstances we could not access.

Being with a soulmate means that you are attracted to each other, rather than to sizes and shapes of certain body parts. You love the whole and laugh at the old concept of dissecting and calling it love. In making love with your soulmate, lust is gone and bliss is realized. There are levels of sexual pleasures that cannot be attained until one has been cleared of guilt, anger, and shame. If you are filled with ghosts from the past, you cannot have a kundalini experience during or after lovemaking.

Sex can be the most empty and hollow of human experiences or the most rapturous and divine. With a soulmate there is such a comfort in being together. There is nothing to prove, no conquest to be won, and no fear of abandonment. You truly can relax and allow the tantric energy to be released. During times of sacred union, all the energy wheels or chakras open, and one becomes aware of the tremendous power within as all these centers spin in ecstasy. This energy literally explodes in the major energy wheels. It's like the most intense light switch being flipped on from the root of your being and the electricity traveling up past your heart to the crown of your head. This pulsating energy will fill you with light and warmth, and flood you with love.

Yin and Yang

In experiencing holy sex, each partner has been healed to such an extent that the recessive male energy of the woman is balanced with her female essence, and the recessive female energy of the man is balanced with his male essence. In the ancient Tao, this balance of male and female energy is depicted as a circle divided into two equal halves by a curved line that makes each half look like a water droplet. Within the largest section of each half is a small circle symbolizing a tiny circle of male energy within the female half and a tiny circle of female energy within the male half of the symbol. This balance is called yin (female) and yang (male).

In the union of two healed (or at least healing) lovers, the healing of the soul results in a balance of these inner forces so that the female is no longer seeking a male to complete the missing piece of her yin/yang. And the male partner has given life to his soft, caring, open, nurturing feminine side and is also feeling complete within himself.

When two lovers are complete in this way, the woman can be strong and powerful, as well as soft, tender, and gentle. The man can be expressive and talk about his feelings, cry, and be vulnerable, in addition to manifesting his usual strength, intellect, and drive. When two such balanced lovers come together, there is no grasping from the man to suck feminine energy from the woman, no grasping from the woman to extract the man's masculine energy. Because each is already complete, their energies are set free to experience remarkable heights of bliss and delight.

Such lovers are already experiencing their own completeness, so when they open sexually and unite, the stars really do move as these powerful spiritual beings join in lovemaking. Imagine the Olympic gods making love, and you can begin to glimpse this reality.

Focusing on the Heart

Here is an exercise in which you can engage before, during, and after making love. It is to be done by both partners. Generally women report that it is easier for them to do, but men with focused attention and practice can be just as successful. What you do is really quite simple, and it can open your entire field of being to a high level of passion and bliss.

Much of this book has been a guide to moving your focus from your head into your heart. Now I'm going to teach you how to move your focus while making love from the genitals into the heart. Let me assure you that, while it isn't easy, it can be done. It's a matter of becoming attuned to the movement of our energy fields, taking a step beyond just the physical body.

Here's the technique: When you and your partner first embrace as you move toward lovemaking, shift your focus from your head and from your sexual organs into the area of your heart. In fact, you can practice doing this right now as you read this section. Until you are accustomed to doing it, you might want to practice with your eyes closed. Take a deep breath and exhale slowly to relax your body. Now focus on your brain. Next focus on your sexual organs. Then move this energy from your brain into your heart, from your sexual organs into your heart. This visualization process will take some practice before you can bring your lovemaking truly to your heart. After you become comfortable with the process (you will actually feel the energy moving into the area of your heart), then you are ready to experience it during your lovemaking.

When you first attempt this technique, be patient and go slowly. You and your partner will have practiced it alone, but when you begin to use the technique during lovemaking, you will tend to want to make love as you always have. That's where the patience comes in. Be patient with yourself, with your partner. The rewards are worth it.

Your capacity for bliss and holiness in your sexual union is much, much greater when you focus on the heart area than when you focus on the area of your sexual organs. Your deep pleasure will expand far beyond what you used to believe was the ultimate. You may experience a tingling sensation where you hadn't before, waves of energy, incredible warmth, a floating sensation, and profound and blissful peace and love.

Couples have literally seen their energy fields and tiny bursts of light around themselves and in the room when fully engaging their hearts in the lovemaking process. It is more than worth any time it takes to achieve this expanded state.

As one pair of soulmates put it, "The sexual expression between us is totally different than anything we've ever experienced. The difference is not only the totality of the experience, it's not just sexual organs touching, it's like our entire bodies are one, our emotions are one, our feelings are one. There is a communication unspoken between us that raises the entire experience to a different level. There is an unselfishness about our sexual relationship. Afterwards there is a feeling of wonder and total closeness that can last for days. We've found in our holy relationship that sex is an enhancer."

The man continues, "It's an exchange of energy between us. Sometimes I think we don't even have to be together. It's just always there, always present . . . " His thoughts trail off to some warm memory as a glow fills his being. He reaches over and softly touches his wife's arm, and they grin like two little children in love with all of life.

His reflection continues, "I think that sex is only a small part of the chemistry. There is so much more to intimacy than the sexual relationship, which is great and comfortable, warm and wonderful. But that isn't it, that's just one part of it. In my past I went through a bizarre period where I got hooked into the idea that sex is the only thing that validates me as a man and that I had to prove it every day, sometimes more than once a day. It can really make you crazy, and I was pretty crazy over it. By the time I met my wife, it was no longer an issue."

What this man learned through his "crazy" years is that intimacy, holy sex, is not about performance or a scorecard or sex being an issue. He adds more of his clear thoughts on the subject, "Sometimes being together in the quiet is enough. Just being in the moment with no razzmatazz is plenty. Nothing needs to be planned around it. It's just being together."

In interviewing couples about their sexual relationship and how it fits into their spirituality, I have found that the men are actually very clear in their thinking. Another man, Alexander, said, "Sex can be an enhancer to love, but I've come to understand that sex has nothing to do with love. It has taken me a long time to learn that. I used to think they were synonymous, but I have finally learned that sex is just a fun adjunct to love."

Holy sex, as described by soulmates and as I have experienced it myself, has been called a sacred moment frozen in time. Everything stops. The whole world appears to stop, and there is this incredible moment of floating. Others experience soaring and a burst of energy that lifts them right out of their bodies. It is this energy that soulmated couples keep referring to. For many, it is huge and all-absorbing; for others, it is quiet floating on an ocean of bliss. For all, it is totally fulfilling and an enhancer of their love lives.

Several soulmated couples have shared with me that, although they can no longer enjoy intercourse because of physical illness, their level of total intimacy has remained constant. They have discovered that simply lying naked facing each other and breathing deeply in harmony while embracing can lead to exquisite joys at this juncture of their lives. No matter what our age or physical challenges, if we are willing to come from our essence of love, then love will find a way to link us together in a holy union.

Under such circumstances, couples have found fulfillment in ways that in years past they would not have considered
sexual. Yet they have discovered that their sexual energy can
flow and express itself fully even when the body is limited. They
have remembered that the soul always remains unlimited.

Betty's husband, Jerry, became permanently impotent as a
result of surgery for prostate cancer, but the two of them have
found new ways to love each other. Jerry considered having an
implant, talked it over at length with Betty, even discussed it
with several surgeons. Then, together, they decided against it.
They made the decision out of love, taking into consideration
the further health risk to Jerry, who was fortunate to be alive.
Betty and Jerry know that their love life is complete and holy.
They experience a sense of bliss they never had while "all their
parts" were still functioning.

Soulmates in loving relationships are always willing to
discover what will work for them and what is pleasing to their
partner.

Elizabeth describes her loving encounters as "an unreal,
invisible, otherworldly kind of feeling. Just all feeling. There's
no awareness of body parts. There's no awareness of being in
the room or of being in the bed or anywhere. It's just an overwhelming, incredible sensation. It doesn't happen every time,
and that's okay. It's not an issue, but when it happens it's mar-
velous."

At another time Elizabeth recalls becoming aware of a
tremendous energy that she is sending out. This field of energy
extends from her and connects with her soulmate's spirit while
they are joined in lovemaking. Elizabeth explains, "I can hardly
look at it because it's so fierce. It's not a bad fierceness. It's just
so intense that it's like God coming together."

The ecstasy of lovemaking between soulmates extends way beyond physical pleasure. The soulmates who have shared their experiences with me speak of the sacredness of their unions. They recall a sense of being lifted out of and above the body. They describe the profound silence of a total surrender, not only to the experience, but to Divine Love. They nearly all speak of truly touching a sense of their oneness. Says one woman, "Sometimes there is no division. I don't know if this remarkable feeling of love is coming from me or from him."

In order to experience holy sex, many have found it helpful to write out and then burn any puritanical concepts about sex that they may have carried, such as: Good girls don't enjoy it. Sex is a duty. Sex is dirty. It's wrong to want sex too often.

Spend some quiet time alone or with your partner and make a game out of it. List any and all rigid beliefs you've carried about experiencing sexual pleasure. Together you can turn the negative beliefs into positive affirmations, such as:

Negative Beliefs

Good girls don't enjoy it.

Sex is a duty.

Sex is dirty.

Positive Affirmations

Empowered women love it, and I am an empowered woman.

Sex is a joy and always pleasurable.

Sex is an expression of my divine self. All my sexual relationships are holy, healthy, and fulfilling.

Other affirmations could be: "The more I allow myself to enjoy sex, the more pleasure my partner and I receive." "My spirit soars to new heights as I allow my sexual energy to come alive." "All my sexual unions are now holy."

As one very loving soulmated couple recounted their experience of profound moments of bliss, I recalled an exercise that I learned during a particularly phenomenal seminar I attended. Dr. Jean Houston shared the program with Dr. Joseph Campbell, the great master of myth. David and I sometimes use this exercise in our workshops, and we find that nearly all participants are deeply moved by the experience.

It is a wonderful exercise to do with your soulmate, but it can have just as profound an impact when done with a close friend or relative. Here is what you do.

In two chairs facing each other, you and your partner sit knee to knee. Gently hold hands while you relax and gaze into each other's eyes. Really "see" each other. After several moments, you each speak simultaneously, saying, "I am _____," inserting your partner's name. For example, if David and I were doing this, he would say, "I am Joan Gattuso." At the same time I would be saying, "I am David Alexander."

It is important that you speak simultaneously rather than taking turns. Be sure to say the full name. At first, it seems very odd to look into the eyes of someone you love and affirm that you are he or she. Once that initial disorientation ceases (one to two minutes), the energy and awareness between the two of you build. Then there comes an opening into a whole new level of awareness as you enter into a state of oneness for a holy instant. It is profound.

Other soulmates speak of having moments while making love of truly feeling God's presence. "It is a spiritual thing." Says another, "Sometimes it's so profound I cry."

Reports Stuart, "At times I experience our lovemaking as spiritual. Sometimes it's more of a physical experience, but whichever it may be, it is always an expression of love." Stuart pauses and reflects, "That perhaps *is* spiritual. Since being with Mary, I can't imagine having sex without love. When I was younger and played around, a lot of sex was strictly a physical thing, but now it's moved way beyond that."

Holy sex may be experienced along with an orgasm, but it is so much more than an orgasm. It is as if your spirits and souls are climaxing above your physical bodies.

It is knowing bliss.

It is how we all can live in relationship when we understand that we are worthy, that we are deserving. Here love holds all meaning. It is in a holy relationship that we each fulfill a divine plan for the healing of the world. Our love heals not only each other but countless other souls as well. Many people have told David and me that our relationship has uplifted and inspired them. So, too, will your relationship be a blessing unto the world.

Soulmated Couples I Have Known and Loved

It is so true that we see in life what we expect to see. Or as my friend Wayne Dyer turned the phrase in the title of his excellent book, *You'll See It When You Believe It*. The more I believed in the miracles and wonders that were possible in relationships, the more I saw those wonders occurring in my own life and in the lives of many others.

A relationship revolution seems to be happening as more and more couples transform and heal their pasts and join together in ways that differ completely from the ways in which they were raised and instructed. There are conscious couples today who refuse to live in the status quo or to accept the norms of their parents and friends. Rather, they are choosing to live in transformative holy relationships.

This is exciting not only for these happy couples but for everyone. They bring to the world the elevated consciousness of what is truly possible. What one couple achieves, all who truly desire it can achieve. The ways of love work, not just for David and me, but for those loving couples whose stories I'm delighted to share.

Marian and Don

Marian and Don met when she was still in college and was hired by Don as an assistant. Don was married to his second wife at the time and was twenty-nine years Marian's senior. Their early relationship was solely a professional one of mutual respect and regard. Through the years of working together, their connection, which was always present on a professional level, began to deepen on a personal level *after* Don's divorce.

Marian left Don's business to work at a large, prestigious firm. In a few years she traveled up the corporate ladder until she was third in command. Her relationship with Don continued to ascend an invisible ladder as well.

Their love for and commitment to each other was total, although they never married. Don carried the soul belief that marriage just was not going to work for him. In view of his track record, he was afraid that marriage could somehow alter the bliss of his relationship with Marian. This he was unwilling to risk. Marian never gave up her desire to be married to Don. She teased him until the day he died that in his next life he would marry her first and that it would be his only marriage.

Yes, Don did become ill, very ill, with cancer. He lost his ability to speak, but he never lost his ability to love Marian. Their devotion and the holiness of their relationship inspired everyone who was privileged to know them. It has been four years since Don's leaving this earth plane, and Marian reports that she still feels and senses his presence constantly.

Although she is in her thirties, she has not dated or in any way sought another relationship. She knows she isn't ready. "I feel like I would be cheating on Don. He is still so much a part of my life. I'm just not ready yet. Someday I will be, but not yet."

Even the appearance of death cannot sever the bond of soulmates.

Sandy and Burleigh

Sandy is a colleague of mine who prayed to attract her soul-mate while living in a remote part of the Pacific Northwest. The following is an excerpt from a letter she wrote me:

> When we were in school I had heard so many horror sto-ries about ministers becoming involved with congregants of the opposite sex that I decided (given my track record with relationships) that it probably would not be a good idea for me. I believed that if "Mr. Right" came through my door I'd send him to the Presbyterian church down the street.
>
> I arrived in Port Angeles in September of 1988 and decided very quickly that I did not want to do ministry alone. I began praying for my perfect mate, telling God that if He was ready to send this person to me, I was ready to receive. My prayer partners (longtime residents of Port Angeles) all chuckled and assured me that I would not find this "perfect spiritual mate" in Port Angeles. Indeed, the outer appearances seemed to support their cynicism.

Through the months of October and November I continued with my request for my "perfect spiritual mate."

The Sunday before Thanksgiving of that year Burleigh showed up in our church. I had met a friend of his at the hospital just a week or two before, and she invited him to join her some Sunday because "he'd really like the minister." There he was, standing next to the bookstore with his shy little Burleigh grin, and I recognized him immediately . . . and ran in the other direction!

He kept coming back (his friend returned to the Catholic church), and in January he joined our new members' class and volunteered for a remodeling job at the church. As we began to talk, our shyness with each other was quickly overcome. We had so much in common with regard to our spiritual journeys.

Burleigh had been living in Forks, Washington, a tiny, isolated lumber town about seventy miles west of Port Angeles. He had just sold his house and was moving to Port Angeles for a short time before heading south. I teased him that God had kept him safely tucked away in the deep woods until I arrived, then tapped him on the shoulder and said, "I got her as far as Port Angeles. I know this girl won't come to Forks." While not crazy about the idea of living in such a tiny, rural village like Port Angeles, there seemed to be nothing that could stop me from being there.

My resolve to never date someone in the congregation went out the window. But then my "resolve" was merely my will. As always, God had something more wonderful in mind. Actually, if the truth be told, we never really "dated." We simply fell in love, let go, and let God.

The individual life paths of soulmates may vary greatly, although there are characteristics that are constant.

I know many couples who are in blessed unions with their soulmates. To reach this point, though, a great number of them had to experience early marriages that ended in divorce and required much healing. Others met at young ages and just knew. They married young and have spent years living in love together. For some it was easy. For others it took much work and many unfulfilled relationships.

Jack and Rosemary

It is truly a joy to observe soulmates in action. Rosemary and Jack are such a radiant, vibrant couple. They met when she was quite young, only fifteen, and a sophomore at the high school from which Jack had graduated as a football hero.

Jack tells of first spotting Rosemary when he noticed her watching him play baseball. After the game he observed her walking home, and soon he began to park his car in front of her house when he needed to go to the store a block away. Jack was hoping that Rosemary would spot his car and come out on her front porch to say hello. That's exactly what happened.

Rosemary says she knew at age fifteen when she had her first date with him that Jack was the man she was going to marry. Recalls Jack, "I knew I would marry her the first time I saw her after the ball game." They waited until Rosemary was twenty-one and Jack was twenty-six to be married, until they had saved enough money to buy a little house.

Both speak of the importance in their lives of God and their religious faith. According to Rosemary, "It's such a part of us. We pray all the time, when we need God and when we don't need Him." They attend Catholic mass daily and pray the rosary together every morning. Says Jack, "It kind of keeps you together a little bit."

When I suggested to them that they are soulmates, neither one was familiar with the term. When I explained it, they agreed it was true. Rosemary said, "You've made a good point. I believe it."

Like all soulmates I interviewed who are living in a holy union, Rosemary and Jack don't work on their relationship. "It's just there," Jack says. "We really don't think about it much. We always make our relationship a priority."

Rosemary and Jack recently celebrated their fiftieth wedding anniversary. I've known them since I was seven. They were wonderful then and inspired me as a child, and they are even more wonderful and inspiring now. They are alive, clear, sincere, happy, and loving. They are amazing!

Donna and John

Donna and John met when she was a bank hostess who traveled from branch to branch opening new offices and he was in the bank's public relations department. John had recently returned to his hometown after graduate school and time in the army. Donna was just out of high school and viewed John, who was twenty-seven, as a much older man.

John remembers their beginning: "I had never wanted to get married. I changed my mind, and it didn't take long. It was like I had known her a long time. It happened really soon for me, right away, after two or three dates." During their first date, he asked Donna for her phone number and wrote it on a piece of paper. Twenty-nine years later, he still carries that piece of paper in his wallet.

Donna says that from the beginning, "I felt safe in our relationship, like I could say anything and be myself and be completely safe." She speaks of their union in terms of reincarnation: "I think we've been together lots of lifetimes. I think of us as helpmates. We just really balance each other." Donna uses the familiar analogy of life being a roller coaster with its ups and downs. But, she says, she doesn't see their life like that, but rather as a teeter-totter, with the two of them balanced in the middle instead of teetering on either end. Both speak of having their own natural rhythm balancing the other: if one is feeling a little off, the other is right on.

They laughingly relate the story of how Donna's father was concerned about her dating an older man. He asked his daughter what John's intentions were. So, on a date that night, Donna boldly asked, "John, just what are your intentions?" John only hesitated slightly as he responded, "Well, to take you out to dinner." Not long afterward, they became engaged.

Donna and John have been married twenty-seven years, and they express much joy in their relationship. I know them well enough to know that they have had times of absolute hell. They lost a daughter who was but seven days old, at a time when there was very little understanding of the impact on the parents of the death of a newborn. Says Donna, "It strengthened our relationship. It made it more mature and deepened our commitment."

In 1990 John, a dedicated daily jogger, had a stroke that left him unable to walk or talk, or even remember his name. Donna recalls how terrifying that time was, but they both had a tremendous commitment to each other and faith in God's goodness. "The commitment became self-empowering. When

John was sick, I was so committed to him and so willing to do whatever I needed to do. In the doing I became completely empowered, because at first I didn't think I could do all the caretaking. For me to go through this when John was really rendered a child was so powerful for me. My self-esteem climbed. I really handled life!"

Although the doctors said it wouldn't happen, through that commitment and much prayer, John began to return to his former self. After four years, he is once again healthy and whole. "Although this is a throwaway society," says Donna, "we know neither one of us is a throwaway commodity."

Because of their high level of commitment, they both feel safe even when they are arguing. How do they disagree? Donna relates, "For me, once you commit to the relationship, it makes it safe for both of you because then you do or say whatever is necessary to clear things up." Adds John, "Our relationship is never involved." They *never* make disparaging comments to each other when they disagree.

They do have moments during arguments when their perceptions are not so clear. As Donna remarks, "We may point at each other, but we quickly realize that doesn't work. So then we work on ourselves." John says, "We work on ourselves, because we bring ourselves to the relationship." Donna continues, "What does work for me is to work on myself. Then I change and disagreements vanish."

Donna and John have grown through the years in their commitment. They have successfully and consciously reared three children, given greatly of themselves to the teens at our church, and used their inner strength and faith to move through John's tremendous health challenge. They live out of their commitment in love with each other.

Jacquie and Peter

Jacquie and Peter met when they participated in a self-growth weekend workshop. They were paired in an exercise and instantly began to sense that something more was happening. They spent much of that first weekend together, working on themselves and connecting with each other. Both felt overwhelmed by what had occurred and found it a bit challenging to process the experience fully.

They lived nearly a thousand miles apart, and Jacquie had returned home before Peter. A psychiatrist, she went to her office the next day, saw ten patients, and began to question what had happened over the weekend. "So I called the airport thinking, maybe I can catch him before he flies home. I just wanted to hear his voice and recapture the feeling that this had really happened. I had already moved back into my routine, and I absolutely thought that I had probably made the whole thing up."

Meanwhile, Peter was at the airport talking to a friend while waiting for his flight. He put his hand in his pocket, pulled out the business card Jacquie had given him, and looked at it for the first time. "I yelled, 'She's a doctor!' If I had known she was a doctor I would never have approached her. I just wouldn't go anywhere near anyone like that. Then I began to get on the plane and I heard myself being paged. I answered the page and the voice on the other end said, 'Was this really real?' I answered, 'Yes, it was.' (Be still my heart!) I could have flown that plane home myself I was so happy."

Peter says that he rambled on and on during that phone conversation. After acknowledging to Jacquie that their encounter was real, he blurted, "It was wonderful and such a great weekend and I love you, and do you know you're a doctor?"

Jacquie quickly adds: "It works both ways. I've got this thing about not wanting anyone, *anyone,* to know I'm a doctor. Anyone who knows I'm a doctor won't even want to know me."

Jacquie's being a doctor made no difference, for this couple has an incredible bond. Peter says that after meeting Jacquie, "It was smooth. There was no getting used to each other. We just clicked. Now that we are together, it's like we've never been apart. There's never been another life. There's never been another marriage."

In Jacquie's view, "If I hadn't had this experience, and someone had said that to me, I would have said, 'Oh, sure!'" After a second divorce, she says, she had abandoned her dreams of such ease and love within a relationship. "To be with the person you want to be with the most in the world, to be with your best friend, that is really the fairy tale. That truly surpasses all the magic in the world . . . and I get to be with him."

Adds Peter, "I love Jacquie very much, but I like her, too. She's my friend. I think you have to like somebody to get into loving them. It's easy with Jacquie. She's such a likable person. I never have to perform for her. I never have to be anything I'm not. I love Jacquie more than—I just can't put words to it. It just wells up in my heart." It also welled up in Peter's eyes, as well as in Jacquie's, David's, and mine as we talked with them. Their love is so total it filled the room.

Peter says that he and Jacquie regularly ask each other, "Is everything okay?" He continues, "Every once in a while a shadow comes between the two of us. Some people would imagine, Well, she's cooled off. She doesn't really love me. It must be something I've said or done. But Jacquie and I have learned to simply ask the question, 'Is everything okay?' Then everything is fine again, everything is cleared up. She's there for me, and I'm there for her. It's give-and-take all the time."

That simple question is a most helpful way to keep the energy clear and to stay connected. Jacquie and Peter share an understanding that whatever is going on is *never* about the other person. Peter relates, "I have been able to grow to where I am really comfortable in this relationship. I accept me because you accept me so much. I feel so grateful because something has developed in me that could not have developed without you. If I begin to feel you are distancing yourself, maybe 1 percent may be because you are acting in a slightly different way. But 99 percent is the projection of my fear."

Jacquie and Peter are soulmates who found each other at midlife. They delight in their love and the constant discovery of what is possible for them individually and as a couple because of their love.

Liz and Hank

Liz and Hank are clear mentally and emotionally about who they are individually, as a couple, and as parents in an extended family. Both were married before, Hank twice and Liz once. They knew what didn't work.

Hank shares his perception of their relationship: "What showed up for me in my relationship with Liz is that there are no issues. There's no withholding. There's no need for us not to be able to share absolutely anything and everything immediately. We tell the whole truth as quickly as possible. It really works for us."

Hank continues, "It's just so different from anything else I've ever had. In my previous relationships, the woman had to be much younger than me, had to have a certain look, had to do certain things, had to be a certain way. With Liz none of that makes any difference at all. It's so clear to me that we're supposed to be together."

The way these two soulmates handle issues that do come up is to understand, according to Liz, that "the issues relate to our past, so we're able to coach each other very gently but directly without a hidden agenda going on, and we quickly clear up whatever it is."

I asked them to elaborate on how coaching works for them. Hank began by stressing that the coaching is reciprocal and that "there's no right or wrong. We don't make the other wrong or have to be right ourselves. It's merely sharing: 'This is what I see, and I'm stepping away from where you are. So take it and use it as you see fit, but I have no agenda around it. I have no issue around it. I have no judgment around it. It's just what I see.' I see her in a struggle, for example, and I want to try and help by sharing myself in that way."

We can all learn from the coaching technique used by Hank and Liz.

Like so many soulmates I have known, these two express their total comfort with each other and their almost instant familiarity when they first met. Says Hank, "There was a sense we had been together for a really long time. That sense was there from the start of our relationship. It embodied comfort, knowing, trust, an unconditionalness of the love between us."

Liz adds, "Our relationship frees me up to explore other things without the relationship being a concern. It's a freedom we have given each other so that we can pursue family, career, spiritual interests, academia, or whatever without the thought that Hank might be angry, might want his dinner on the table. I see other people around me often concerned about what I would call petty things, and as a result other areas of growth aren't addressed. The person's focus is about so-and-so's quirks and whether or not he'll be annoyed."

Hank jumps in: "The soulmate feeling for me has to do with being aware of who we are in the relationship and also being aware that we each have a lot of history. We absolutely honor the fact that we have a lot of history and neither one of us has anything to do with what shows up out of that history."

Hank explains that when the old stuff (history) is showing up for one partner, the other partner will ask: "Is this something out of your history?" Their process continues with one of them next saying something like, "I'm here for you. Tell me what you need. I'm not going to guess. I'm not going to pretend I know better than you do."

I love the story of how Liz and Hank met at an *est* weekend, did some sharing there, but didn't see each other again until a year later at a party. Liz needed a ride home and Hank obliged, calling her the next day and asking her to go to a seminar with him. After that seminar he drove her home again, began to stop over at Liz's home regularly, and never left. "I stayed for life," grins Hank.

Of all the soulmated couples I know, Hank and Liz have the most remarkable relationship with their extended family, which includes Joe, the man to whom Liz was married for seventeen years and the father of her three boys.

Early in their relationship Liz and Hank realized that if her three sons were to grow up in a healthy, stable, loving environment, their father had to remain a vital part of their lives. Accomplishing that consciously, mindfully, and lovingly, without any party feeling threatened, became their goal.

The two of them realized, in Liz's words, that "We could have a life of tremendous conflict if the boys weren't comfortable with all three adults." They all three came to realize that egos had to be set aside. And that is exactly what they did. What has followed I view as truly remarkable and a living testimony to the results that can be obtained when parents are emotionally and spiritually mature enough to stay focused on the well-being of the children. When this occurs, the extended family can live in a state of peace and integrity, in a huge, open space, rather than in conflict, upset, struggle, and narrowness.

Hank says he now counts Joe among his best friends, and Liz immediately chimes in and says she does as well: "We do everything involving the boys together. We go places. We share the cars. We co-coach soccer."

Liz's designer-sweater business calls for her to do a great deal of weekend travel to art shows, and Hank leaves his law practice behind to assist her. When they are out of town, Joe stays with his sons in Hank and Liz's home—gladly—asking only, "Will you be home by dinner?" Says Liz, "It's so easy. It supports everyone." Hank agrees, adding, "It's what happens when you have 100 percent, unconditional commitment to each other. We are unconditionally committed to each other— absolutely. Whatever happens happens, and we are still committed."

The holy relationship that Hank and Liz share is large enough to embrace not only her three sons and her former husband but also Hank's three grown children and his former spouses. They set a remarkable example of what is possible when love is more important than anything else.

Kathy and Dick

Kathy and Dick's marriage is the second for each. Kathy, now the mother of two young children and a couples seminar leader, describes their relationship as "on a different plane than most people are used to. Not that we're better than other couples, just different. It's not a utilitarian kind of relationship where your communication is at a level of just talking about practical things. It's much deeper than that. It's on a spiritual level."

She continues: "You have to be whole and then come together. We have, individually, a really close relationship with God. To me, being with a soulmate is like loving someone from the inside out."

Dick, a psychologist, elaborates: "I wouldn't doubt that we've crossed paths before and will continue to do so in the future."

Kathy jumps in, sharing her feelings upon first encountering Dick: "As I approached him [she was in a theatrical review and engaging the members of the audience], I thought, Oh, I've known this person before. I knew that night when I sat down with Dick. I just knew."

Dick seems pleased at hearing Kathy's words and asks her, "How did that make you feel?"

She responds, "Secure, really secure."

Describing their relationship, Kathy says they are like interlocking pieces of a puzzle in many ways. For example, "He has a natural gift for listening, and I have a natural gift for talking. I look at him like a gift from God. Our life together is a gift from God."

Kathy explains further: "Part of being a soulmate is having a really positive vision of the other person and of the relationship. Dick could see things in me that I couldn't see. I could see things in him that he couldn't see. We built each other up, and we still do that."

Adds Dick, "Before we met, the years of my life—the tough times, the depression, the trauma, the loss—were in preparation for our relationship. I was just ready for it to happen. I had a knowing that there's got to be more to it than the upset. There's got to be a deeper, better level of connection, understanding, and support. I also knew there was more to spirituality than going to church. I had this knowing inside that there was a lot more cooking in me, and I was searching for it. I didn't put together the idea of spiritual existence with a soulmate until later."

Kathy's experience with what I call "the knowing" was very similar to mine. In describing her first marriage, she says: "I knew I was in trouble walking down the aisle. My father knew. Isn't that an awful thing? I didn't listen to my inner voice."

Kathy continues, "I think in order to have a healthy relationship or a soulmate relationship, you have to be spiritual or at least traveling on the same plane. Otherwise, you go through the motions, but there's always an emptiness."

Bill and Julianne

Bill and Julianne are an absolutely adorable young couple from my congregation. Last year Bill, a student in a large class I was teaching, set goals that he wanted to achieve as a result of applying the spiritual principles being taught through this twelve-week class.

Bill's primary goal was to meet his soulmate and to be in a holy relationship. He certainly was one of the brightest stars in that class, and his glee was infectious. Bill sums up his philosophy after having met his soulmate and knowing he wanted her to be his wife, "I'm going to work on myself and love her."

Julianne describes where she was emotionally when she and Bill met. She had spent three years learning about herself, "but I never really looked inside. I was a person who always looked outward. After doing a lot of recovery work, I had determined that the common denominator in all my bad relationships was me. I was the only person I could really look at. There was nowhere else to point the finger. Bill opened a door for me to find out what it is like to be able to share and express opinions, to blossom, to push past my fears, to open up and say things."

Julianne and Bill live out of the core belief that they "can always have joy" in their relationship. According to Bill, "There can always be peace. There can always be serenity. My only job in this relationship is really just to love Julie. I don't have to change her. I don't have to fiddle around with who she is. My only job is to love her unconditionally. In addition to that, my job is to work on myself."

Julianne, like so many young women, had no firsthand experience of what a good relationship would look like. "I was reading books that said things like: get a picture of what it is you like. I read some really awful books on relationships that would focus on the physical description. It was more or less related to genetics and what our children would look like versus what the relationship would feel like. I had no friends who talked about what their relationships felt like. They were all in bad to rotten relationships. There was a lot of anger in these women. There was a lot of anger in their relationships. They would talk about how lousy men were and how lousy their relationships were. I felt like I was listening to them because we were friends, but inside it didn't ring true."

As Julianne began to separate herself from this all-too-common attitude, "I read every book on relationships I could find. I built a very strong relationship with God. I did a lot of praying and soul-searching to determine my core essence and what I need to work on. I became willing to share feelings."

One thing Julianne discovered on her journey of emotional and soul recovery was that she wasn't even sure what a feeling was—she had to learn through the support of a loving group. Through inner work, she came to recognize her own unhealed anger. "I wanted to give up at that point because I thought, This is the worst thing that someone can be—angry. I learned appropriate ways to let my anger out. That's when I started to be more open. I switched almost all my friends. I could no longer be with those angry, angry women. Then I started meeting new people who were in a different place."

When I ask Bill and Julianne about their coming together and being soulmates, Bill says, "When Julie showed up, I had my eyes open and I recognized her for who she was. Julie felt safe. She had this presence about her that was very powerful. I truly believe that in all the relationships I have, that as long as I take responsibility for everything I want, I can create them exactly as I want. A concept that I have a lot of faith in is that as human beings we have these magnets that we put on ourselves, and what I want to attract will be drawn to me by these magnets. So if what I want is safety and a relationship that is nurturing, then I put on my safety and nurturing magnets and attract that out of Julie. I can't force her into becoming nurturing and creating safety for me. However, if that's the space I'm coming from, it will be, in and of itself, attractive to her own traits of nurturing and safety."

I asked Bill and Julianne how they feel when skeptics project their cynicism onto this expressive and happy couple, saying such things as, "Yeah, right, life will always be such joy and bliss." I found Bill's answer intriguing. "When I hear that from others, it's a motivator for me." He pauses. "Wait a minute! I think, I'm not letting my light shine brightly enough!" He continues, "I know I create everything I get, and everything that I have gotten has been my responsibility in terms of my reaction and my perceptions. Whatever it is I'm putting out is not clear enough for others to understand. If I'm getting their negativity back, I must not be making it clear enough. So such attitudes just redouble my efforts. Like, let me think of some other way that I can word it, or say it, or show it, or demonstrate it, so that they can get it and give up those old negative attitudes about relationships."

Bill and Julianne know that loving each other unconditionally serves them and in turn all that they encounter as they move through life together living in love.

Felicia and Luis

Some soulmated couples are racially mixed. What I have found most interesting and amazing among the ones I have known is that they attract no outside prejudice. This is clearly a reflection of their great inner acceptance and love.

Felicia, the administrative assistant at my church, met her husband, Luis, in college when she was eighteen and he was nineteen. Felicia was reared in an upper-middle-class neighborhood, the youngest daughter in a family of Greek and German heritage. Luis is from the Dominican Republic and is of Indian, Spanish, and African lineage, the youngest of eight children. At age ten he moved to Brooklyn, New York, with his mother and a brother and sister.

Though they came from very different backgrounds, their love of sports would earn both athletic scholarships.

Luis remembers, "The first time I saw Felicia she was just out of high school and at the college checking it out. She was in the workout room lifting weights, and she was so skinny and weak that she couldn't even lift the bar without any weights on it! I felt sorry for her.

"I didn't see her again until a year later and remembered: that skinny girl, I really wanted to date her. I noticed her, but she didn't notice me. I was persistent, though, and finally a friend introduced us. My opening line was, '¿Hablas español?' 'What?' Felicia exclaimed back at me. We began to hang out together, and finally I asked her, 'Are we dating?' She replied, 'Yes, I guess so.'"

Says Felicia, "I was drawn to Luis's sincerity. He wasn't afraid to be himself. We shared common ideals: seeing the good in everyone, going out of our way to help others feel comfortable and good about themselves. We shared a belief in God and that there was a reason for our being together. We both were taught as children: what goes around, comes around. We both live out of the understanding that what we put out, we later draw back into our lives."

Felicia continues, "Our connection is way beyond the physical. It is much deeper than that. From the beginning there was something else. We understood each other."

Adds Luis, "Her personality fit me."

I asked them to share their insights into their families' acceptance.

"In my country," Luis begins, "there aren't so many color or racial barriers. My mom loved Felicia. My mom loved me, and anyone I would love my mom would instantly love."

Says Felicia, "I was raised to respect other races. I never thought of my family as prejudiced, but until I was a senior I kept from them that I was dating Luis. All through college they knew Luis, but thought we were just friends.

"I was afraid I would have to make a choice. Not that I would have to choose between my family and Luis, but I knew I was choosing my 'self,' my highest good, which was the relationship. It would have been devastating if they had rejected me, but my dad asked me, 'Is this what will make you happy?' My parents were afraid society would hurt me."

Luis and Felicia are very clear in their commitment to love and agree that they are unaware of attracting any outside prejudice. They are so comfortable with who they are individually, as a couple, and as a family that any narrow prejudicial thinking doesn't show up in their experiences.

Felicia and Luis now have two adorable daughters (the younger is my godchild, I'm delighted to say) who are being taught that God created everyone equal. No matter how different we are, our differences make us unique and interesting people.

Luis concludes, "I really believe racism comes from people being naive and in their own fear."

Felicia and Luis are an extremely loving couple who followed their hearts and found happiness.

In interviewing these soulmates and knowing many more, I have identified a number of attitudes and characteristics they all share. I offer them to you as guidelines:

Share together in your spiritual life. Walk a similar path.

See your partner as a gift from God.

Unconditionally love and support each other.

Come from a place of gratitude in your relationship.

Recognize the loving essence of the other.

Work on yourself (your partner will do the same). As a result you will experience few ego-backed demands. You won't argue about the inconsequential.

Don't keep score.

Are not given to jealousy.

Don't have "male" jobs or "female" jobs around the house.

Feel secure, safe in every situation.

Love your partner from the inside out.

Hold a high vision of the relationship.

Hold a high vision of your partner.

See life as an adventure, always moving, growing, becoming more.

Have ease of being together, a high comfort level.

Respect your partner's differences.

Give advice only when asked.

Have fun together.

Be open, kind, and loving to all.

Always keep your relationship the top priority.

If you are still seeking your soulmate and very much desire to enter into such a transformative, holy union, here are some further guidelines to consider.

Don't limit God or yourself by believing that your perfect partner has to be from your side of town or within a ten-mile radius. I have heard people say that someone was "geographically undesirable" because the potential partner lived in the next county. Several soulmates mentioned in this book moved across the country to be together. They changed careers, left furniture and pensions behind, to live in love. One couple I know had a long-distance relationship between South Africa and Chicago and are now happily married. Thank God, both of them work for airlines, as the woman still commutes from South Africa to Detroit to catch her flights. If you have ever used "geographically undesirable" as an excuse, it's time to re-examine your priorities.

Soulmates often have many and varied life experiences before coming together. I asked for my soulmate to be of a compatible age. David is eight years older. I'm pleased that he's not twenty-eight years older, but there are soulmated couples where a large age difference is the case. Be open to a much larger picture than you held when you were a teenager.

Soulmates come from all backgrounds, in all shapes and sizes, from all races and nationalities, from all age brackets. What they have in common is that their living comes from the heart. They have made enough of the journey from head to heart to be able to recognize each other when they meet. Their eyes are open. They were ready, and now they are living in love. They are living what they long knew in their hearts was possible. It can happen to you. It's happening now for so many. It happened for me.

Here is *A Course in Love.* Practice what is set forth. Look at your life and history and patterns in depth. Heal. Learn your soul's lessons. Forgive. Wake up. Be open, kind, and loving, and Divine Love will draw to you your perfect partner.

God bless you.

Lectures and Workshops
with Joan Gattuso

Joan Gattuso's writing is equaled and perhaps even surpassed by her inspirational lectures and workshops, which she has given before audiences throughout the United States. Her style is loving, powerful, warm, humorous, motivational, and always entertaining.

People's lives change after they attend Joan's presentations and follow the universal principles she teaches about creating ideal relationships and a happy, fulfilling life.

If you wish information about booking her for a presentation, a schedule of her lectures and workshops, or a catalog of her available tapes, telephone 1–800–2LOVEU2 (256-8382) or write to:

Joan Gattuso Presentations
P.O. Box 22685
Beachwood, OH 44122